AFRICA PRESENTS THE CONGO RDC

And

Mr. Aleyi Atondi

How Can This MAN LIVE WITH HIS IN-LAWS FOR

OVER 15 YEARS?

By

BEPONA COLLECTION

AFRICA presents the CONGO RDC

and

Mr. Aleyi atondi

How Can this man live with his in-laws

for over 15 years?

Printed in the United States of America

BeponaBooks

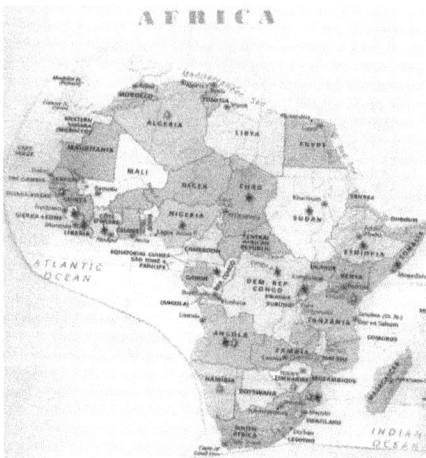

AFRICA

KINSHASA, THE CAPITAL CITY OF THE CONGO

RDC PRIOR TO THE CIVIL WAR

TABLE OF CONTENTS

INTRODUCTION

In essence, African men are well known in terms of their stamina. They are actually known as hardworking individuals. Usually, they are very determined to making their wives happy. They seek all the necessary means to capture the full attention of their wives. On the other hand, women believe that a wife's duty is to remain focused in their homes, and also to make sure that everything is going as it should around the house. This is actually women's strategies in terms of capturing their husband's attention. In fact, the African culture requires that a young man be taught from his early age about his manhood's responsibilities. At the time the boy becomes a man of full age, it is understood that all the cultural instructions received during his younger age, have been imbedded in his mind. Further, it is understood that the man will act accordingly in the society. This in fact is the reason why the African parents strive on training their sons from their early ages. These strategies were developed by their ancestors and eventually the wisdom came from God.

Parents advise their sons, "Remember that a man must be a bread winner in a family." In addition, parents awaken the consciousness of their sons that a lethargic man would never find anybody to marry, because no woman can converge with a man that is not productive in the society. Consequently, the African men always strive to make it, so that they could impress their women in terms of meeting their needs. The main reasons of emphasizing the cultural principle to young men are really to prevent a wife looking elsewhere in order to satisfy her basic needs and occasionally to enjoy some luxury needs. Such behavior would be considered to be a dishonor and degradation to the husband as well as to the society's view, if the wife develops such awful actions.

Regardless to the most popular and important cultural education which Mr. Atondi had basically received since his childhood, the man broke the record of his ancestors' belief. He lost his cultural identity by exhibiting such a peculiar demeanor, which was unacceptable to the Congolese culture.

Mr. Aleyi Atondi was an exceptional Congolese man. Apparently, due to the circumstance he had found himself in at that particular time, he took advantage of developing atypical mannerism. In spite of to the childhood education which he had received from his African parents, Atondi, unfortunately lost his African's stamina, as well as his Congolese man's pride. He appeared skeptical to everyone around him. People became convinced that Atondi had developed such a degree of laziness in less than two years after getting involved with the young lady called Yosika Bala.

Yosika was born from a well to do family, and her parents were very capable of providing for her needs. Evidently, this had been the major motif behind Atondi's sluggishness. Obviously, Atondi had really exemplified a higher degree of laziness in the history of African's men and particularly, in the history of the Congolese men. His lethargy was overwhelming that no word could do justice for expressing it.

Prior to meeting Yosika Bala, Aleyi Atondi was an undergraduate, college student in Kinshasa, the capital city of the Democratic Republic of Congo. He was a junior at that time, and was majoring in Finance. Further, during that time, Atondi was known to many as a well organized, and a hard working gentleman. He was a characteristically an African man who honored his African's culture thoroughly. While he had been a student, he used to combine both, his studies, as well as doing some personal business on the side in order to support himself.

Atondi knew that he did not come from a wealthy family; due to this fact, he was determined to detain his college degree. His goal had been to find a job in the Finance Department in Kinshasa right after graduating from college. Further, Aleyi Atondi used to remind himself, as the old saying, "Where there is a will, there is a way." He had always confirmed that never will he be an admirer of any college graduate, but he would rather do whatever it would takes to become one of them, regardless to his family social status. He really was fascinating with college education. While he was striving to achieve his undergraduate degree, Atondi was renting a small one-bed room apartment from his landlord's property. The landlord was so pleased with him, because he kept the apartment neat and cozy. In fact, Atondi was able to furnish his little apartment with his moderate income. Further, the apartment had all the necessary comfort required including some entertainment devices.

Due to the fact that Atondi was well organized and disciplined, he attracted many friends. He also had several cousins from his extended family that used to travel back and forth from his native village to Kinshasa, the capital, city of the country, for trading activities. All of them had formed the habit of staying at his apartment. In fact, they stayed free of charge while they came to conduct their businesses. Aleyi was indeed a philanthropist as far as his friends and cousins were concerned. In exchange however, Aleyi would give money to his cousins when they were returning to the village in order to purchase certain commodities, which would permit him to create a small business in Kinshasa. This actually was how he made his living while he was an undergraduate student. Aleyi and his classmates adored to repeat the expression, "Do not give me your fish, sir or madam, but rather teach me how to fish." This expression made them very motivated in their school works.

PISODE I

**How Yosika Bala wound up getting too involved with Aleyi
Atondi?**

As far as Miss Bala' s background was concerned,
Yosika felt that Aleyi Atondi did not fit to be her husband or was
not her type of companion at the time that they had accidentally
met at the Central Station. Central Station was known as a main
area where travelers actually made connections or transfers when
going to and from different directions. It was just a matter of
thirty minutes when Yosika Bala and Aleyi Atondi had an
opportunity to exchange a few words.

Aleyi Atondi could not take his eyes off Yosika.
She was gorgeous and was well dressed. Although, her
outfit was simple, it was however with such a refinement.
Her hair was newly braided and the style was outstanding.

In High School, Bala was a senior. She was well aware that the ultimate year in high school would require hard working in order to pass her "Examen d'Etat" or the nationwide high school exam, prior to receiving her high school diploma. Bala was heading to the Nord city which was four hours away from the Central Station, and it was eight hours away by Bus from the City Capital. Atondi on the other hand, was on vacation at that time, in his native village. His village was located approximately twenty minutes away from the Central Station, and it was four hours away from the City Capital by bus. However, on that particular day, as it were, Aleyi had decided to walk to the Central Station in order to conduct some small business activities.

That was actually the day he met Yosika Bala. Miss Bala stood five feet five inches tall, and weighed around one hundred and ten pounds, whereas Aleyi Atondi was exactly five feet tall, and weighed around one hundred thirty five pounds. Prior to expressing his desire to propose to her, Atondi made sure to initially, find out all the necessary information regarding the young lady's family. Further, he was curious to find out whether or not Yosika had any relatives residing in Kinshasa city.

The gentleman was smart enough to also inquire about the boroughs, as well as the home addresses of both of her close relatives living in Kinshasa.

Yosika told Atondi about her Parents, and she unfortunately revealed to Aleyi the type of lucrative business her father was engaged in. Yosika also mentioned to Atondi that she actually had two Aunts living in Kinshasa. She told him that one of them called "Aunt Lesa Bala. She was from her patriarchal side. She also told him that, as far as her aunt's occupation was concerned, she actually had a small business. Further, she told Atondi also that her aunt had signed a small contract with the bread factory. Therefore, she sells bread and corn meals flour at the local market. She concluded in effect that, that was how her aunt actually made her living. Furthermore, Yosika specified also that her aunt was a widow.

In addition, she informed Aleyi that she had another aunt from her matriarchal side, called Esperance Mutema. Aunt Mutema was a high School Teacher at the "Sacre-Coeur Lyceum. Atondi got excited upon hearing that statement. Suddenly, he exclaimed! "I, too, have a cousin who is a Teacher at the same Lyceum. What a coincidence," he exclaimed! Therefore, under that excitement, both of them exchanged information regarding their relatives as well as about themselves. Bala did not write any information about Atondi or her cousin's name, but Atondi did; he did not want to miss the opportunity.

In fact, five minutes before the Bus driver started making the announcement for boarding activity, Aleyi

Atondi whispered to Yosika, "eh listen Yosika, "You are very pretty! I really love you; can I propose to you?" Yosika was somewhat shocked, and had to reply to him emphatically, "Oh, no", I am sorry, currently, that issue is out of my mind. It is not going to be possible.

I am in School right now, and I do not intend to get engaged to any man at the present time. I prefer to remain focused in my studies, because I still have a long way to go." Having said these words to Atondi, Miss Bala departed, and immediately, got on the bus without waiving at Atondi. While she was in the Bus, Miss Bala started to reprimand herself, "I surely made a big mistake. I shouldn't have been so opened to this fellow so quickly. He had probably received the impression that I actually like him, because I had spoken to him in such a kindly manner. He probably had no slightest idea that I was just trying to be courteous.

Well, I am glad that I had given him the right and an emphatic answer. Well, let him deal with it," she said to herself and was later revealed to everyone concerned.

Four hours later, Yosika had finally arrived at her destination. Her uncle and his daughter Kitoko came to pick her up at the bus station. Both cousins were the same age and had gotten along harmoniously. It was quite apropos, because they also went to the same High School, and they were both senior. In addition, both of them were preparing their nationwide or High School examinations during that same year.

Therefore, both cousins have lots of things in common which kept them very close to each other. Her cousin Kitoko asked Bala, "how was her trip?" She replied to her that, "In general everything went well, but you will not believe what happened to me at the Central Station when I was waiting for the bus transfer," she said.

Kitoko replied spontaneously, "Well tell me what had happened?" Bala felt therefore obligated to relate the whole incident about Aleyi Atondi in details. At first, Kitoko noticed that Yosika sighed, prior to beginning the narrative.

Then, she continued, "Kitoko you won't believe the manner in which this young man acted;" At this point, Kitoko got interested in her narrative, and questioned her, "What had he done?" Bala answered, "He actually approached me, and he whispered in my ears, "You are very pretty!" Then right away he continued, saying "Can I possibly propose to you?" Kitoko laughed loud, and added, "What was the matter with that fellow? Had he really come towards you, and asked you something of that sort?" That was weird, of course!" Kitoko told Bala, shaking her head from left to right. Kitoko continued, "You don't even know him, how could he possibly dare rushing to ask you such a big question, Laughter? He probably believed it was love at first side, Kitoko added, giggling." Thus, both of them started laughing their heads off. Then Yosika commented, "Kitoko, based on his appearance, certainly such thing could never happen," she said.

Furthermore, Bala continued "I think my being kind and polite to that fellow had appeared to him as though I were interested in establishing a serious relationship with him. I surely was not." She also concluded that, that fellow was actually untrustworthy as far as she was concerned. She also continued saying, "How could he possibly expect me to consent to his marriage proposal, when he had just met me?

Besides, he talked to me for a very short duration. That did not mean that he knew me well enough to jump to that conclusion!" So, her cousin replied, "Definitely not, that is not knowing a person to whom you should actual propose to marry." Yosika, Kitoko said to her, "You cannot allow yourself to get into that sort of predicament." Bala told Kitoko, "I must remember my mother's advice regarding selecting a man to marry. She always reminds me to shirk such a disastrous destiny, and that is exactly what I will have to do," she told her cousin.

Bala continued, "Kitoko, this fellow actually tricked me, indeed, because he began by exploring information about my family, and about my relatives living in Kinshasa. He did these things prior to expressing his deep feelings about me. In addition, he did not even give me any hint regarding such thing during the entire conversation. Obviously, if he had done it, I would have sensed it; and therefore, I would have never given him my family's private information. Kitoko asked Bala, "Did you actually reveal everything to him about your family and both of your aunts in Kinshasa?" Bala held her fore head, and answered, "Kitoko, I actually did it." Certainly, I do regret it now, for having done it." Her cousin said to her,

Yosika that action was actually unwise on your part. You should not have acted in such unwise manner."

On my part, Kitoko said, "My mother had repeatedly told me that every time you meet a fellow, you must deal with him gradually. You cannot reveal everything about you to him, instantly. Because, remember Kitoko said, at that time, that person is a stranger to you. Your conversation with a stranger should be very reserved, and not to be so open at the first time.

At least this is what my mother had been telling me all along, on a regular basis. Didn't your mother advise you regarding these issues?" Kitoko asked Bala. Bala replied, "Of course my mother, being an intelligent lady, she had mentioned all those tips to me as well. I just happened not to be cautious enough at that time. I guess I was somewhat tired with such a long trip, and my brain was not alert enough at that particular time. Bala added that I really hope he loses the information I had given him." Kitoko said: Surely, if he loses that piece of paper on which he wrote your information, evidently that would be it. He would never be able to connect with you again." Yosika was delighted to hear those words, and she said, well let it be written so, Kitoko, she said to her.

Can you possibly describe that man's appearance to me? Kitoko asked. Bala replied, "Concerning his height, he appears as your domestic Kimueni. Kimueni should be about five feet, right? She verified with her cousin." Kitoko replied, almost so, or a little less than five feet. So, the fellow is not that tall! You are actually taller than he is?" Yes, indeed," Bala replied. Kitoko asked her, "What kind of complexion does he have?" Bala answered that, "Well, actually darker than mine." Regarding the expression of his mouth, Bala specified that, "It looks slightly just like the one of our chemistry instructor." Kitoko, exclaimed! "Oh, so he is not handsome at all! If that gentleman is the way you have described him, I would conclude that Atondi is not fit to be your husband at all, Yosika." Bala replied, Kitoko that is exactly how I felt, and my answer to that question, "Was an emphatic, "No thank you," as soon as he had completed his last word."

Bala continued, Kitoko "I hope Aleyi will not seek to meet my aunts in Kinshasa, in order to tell them about me. Further, I also hope that he will not express his desire to propose to me. I actually say these things because he appeared as though he is an aggressive fellow. " Yosika continued I will be so embarrassed if this man does meet both of my aunts, under the guise that I have recommended him to meet them." Her cousin understood the situation very well, and added, "Yes", Bala you were not cautious at all in giving this fellow your aunts' names as well as their home addresses. If this man does go to meet them, both of your aunts would not hesitate to believe that you actually love this ugly fellow; and that you want him to actually meet them in order to establish further intimate relationship, Kitoko added, shaking her head. Yosika said, as the old saying in French, "L'experience m'a rendue sage", meaning that I have learned from my mistakes!"

Kitoko asked Bala, did you give him our home address here as well? Bala replied, "No, I am glad I did not, because the bus driver had just made the announcement for the passengers to get on board when he had begun expressing his feelings of intimacy. I am pretty sure that would have been the next thing he would have wanted to request. However, I seized that opportunity to run quickly towards the bus stop without even waving at him. While I was in the bus, I watched him standing there immovable until the bus driver had pulled out the bus. He probably began wondering, the reason why I did not wave at him, and avoided to look through the window in his direction. Well, that was actually the indication that I was not looking forward to exploring his relationship any further.

A year later, however, after Yosika had passed her state board exam, and detained her high school diploma, she decided to go to Kinshasa, the city Capital, in order to make college arrangements to pursue her College education.

EPISODE 2

Atondi Meets Yosika Again in Kinshasa

When Yosika had arrived in Kinshasa, she was staying by her aunt Esperance Mutema. She was her mother's youngest sister. Certainly, Aleyi Atondi had preceded her. Further, Atondi had done his best to meet both of Yosika's aunts prior to establishing any sort of relationship with Yosika herself. In addition, not only he had made the first move of meeting her relatives, but he also seized the opportunity to express his desire to both of her aunts about proposing to Yosika. Furthermore, Atondi had gone to pay her cousin a visit at the Lyceum where Yosika's aunt was teaching. Prior to Atondi's visit to Lyceum, his cousin and Esperance Mutema knew each other, because they were co-workers. However, Atondi wanted to strengthen that relationship because of his deep interest in Yosika. Nevertheless, aunt Mutema could never wish Aleyi Atondi to marry her beautiful niece. She was totally reserved when it came to that discussion. In fact, she wondered the reason why Yosika had to recommend Atondi to meet her. Eventually there was something about Atondi that aunt Mutema disliked. What was it really? Probably it was his height or the expression of his mouth, or just the vibrations about him. She could not actually pin-point the cause.

As soon as Aleyi became aware of Yosika's arrival in Kinshasa, he got excited. He decided to pay her a visit at her aunt Mutema's home. Unfortunately, on that day, Bala was invited at her aunt Lesa Bala. He could not see her that day as he had desired. The following day, was a Saturday, Aleyi returned to see whether or not she had come back. He was told that she still has not returned. Aleyi missed her for the second time.

On Sunday, again, Aleyi went back to her aunt Mutema's home. He was again told that Yosika is still at her aunt Bala's place. Aleyi wanted to see Yosika so badly. Therefore, he decided to pay her a visit at her aunt Bala's home, because he had kept her home address as well. When he arrived at aunt Bala's home, he was told that she had just left. She is actually on her way to her aunt Esperance's house. It was too late for Aleyi to travel to that borough on that evening; so he had postponed the visit for another.

Aleyi was not lucky enough to encounter Yosika for quite some times. He was missing her every time he had planned to meet her. A month later, he finally saw her at her aunt Mutema for the first time since she has arrived. Aleyi was delighted to see Yosika again after one whole year since they had met at the Central Station. Atondi's first word was, "Congratulation Yosika, I heard you had passed your state board exam, and that you now had detained your High School diploma. Yosika replied, "Thank you, I had to actually pass the exam because I was well prepared. It could not have been otherwise, because my parents would have been very upset with me, and that is something that I had to prevent, she added.

Atondi could not have wasted time to carry on a conversation with Yosika. He told her that, "I am so glad that I had given me your aunts' home addresses. I could have never been able to see you again, otherwise." He continued, "I really felt badly to notice the manner in which you had suddenly rushed to get on the bus without even waving at me that day, at Central Station. Needless to tell you, how disturbing that view had been to me for quite sometimes. Actually, I had stood there immovable watching the bus pulled away. Further, I had blamed myself for not being fast enough to get your destination address. If I had had your address, I could have established a correspondence with you during the entire past year." In fact, he continued, "I had gone several times to both of your aunts in the attempt to ask for your address, apparently, they were so protective of you. I had probably appeared skeptical to them, as a result, they refrained giving your address.

Yosika got upset and said to him impulsively, "Aleyi, you should not have done that. I had no idea that the reason you actually had wanted to possess my relatives' address was to start visiting them at their homes without my permission." Aleyi was somewhat embarrassed to hear this complaint. Finally, he replied, "I did not mean any harm Yosika."

Bala then said to Atondi, "I wonder how did each one of my aunts reacted to your unexpected visit?" She asked. Aleyi said to her, "Well, I had actually noticed that your aunt Lesa Bala was nicer than your aunt Esperance. Further, Atondi said that it is bizarre, because my cousin and your aunt are co-workers, and therefore, our communication would have been easy and pleasant, and yet, your aunt appeared so reluctant to discuss the topic regarding relationship between you and myself. In fact, it is easy to just pick up those negative vibrations from her, based on the way she actually swifts the conversation and the variation of her tone of voice, so to speak.

Bala replied, "Aleyi in reality, you have been too fast. You do not really proceed in such an abrupt manner. Atondi said to her, "I actually meant what I had said to you at the Central Station, if you still recall it Yosika. I think it bears to reiterate it sometimes. In fact, I do recall you answering me, "No, I cannot marry you." Bala replied, yes indeed, that is exactly what I had said to you, and in fact, the explanation was given to you thoroughly. Even though it was a short answer, but it was precise. It was necessary for me to give you that explicit answer. It is quite obvious that I wouldn't want to commit myself at this time." Atondi, whispered again, Yosika, please do not say that, because I really have made up my mind to marry you. It should be no problem now that you have received your high school diploma. I think it should be fine," he said. Yosika replied angrily, "Aleyi, if I were a man like you, who is seeking to marry a young lady, I would never marry a lady who had given me a negative answer right there and then.

The reason that the lady promptly gave you a negative answer to your marriage proposal meant actually a great deal. I believe that it would be wise not to seek further explanation. Further, attempting to dig deep could cause frustration to the other party. Believe me she said, sometimes it is better to hear just a few words than several words at the same time." Bala continued, "Please, I would appreciate it very much if you would stop forming the habit of visiting me at my aunts' homes. Certainly, your visits would result drastic effects around my aunts' homes. Consequently, they would be forced to complaint about my behaviors to my parents. I would not want to create any unpleasant situations between my aunts, my parents, and myself. You now have my honest answer regarding this matter. Please, do not resume questioning me on this subject any longer. If I may reiterate, I am here to pursue my college education. I am not seeking to settle down." In effect, you should remember that a serious relationship cannot be forced, but it must come naturally and harmoniously," Yosika told Atondi in a very calm voice.

Atondi grew quiet, and repeated, congratulation anyway for your school achievement. Having said this, he decided to leave, bidding everybody goodbye. Naturally, he was frustrated for being turned down.

Yosika was finally admitted in college, and was majoring in law. She was a freshman and Atondi was senior. He was majoring in finance. For the first few months, Atondi and Yosika did not have any opportunity to talk, but occasionally one of them would have an opportunity to glance in one direction without saying a word. One day however, aunt Mutema and her husband happened to drive around the College Campus where Yosika and Atondi were studying. It was around 4:30 P.M., and that was almost the time Yosika's classes ended. Therefore, the couple picked her up that day. As they began driving, and as soon as they had arrived close to the bus stop, they perceived Atondi standing alone at the bus station with his school bag.

Apparently, he had just missed the bus. The weather appeared as though it was going to rain. The wind was blowing hard and the sky was turning darker. Aunt Mutema recognized Atondi as Belinda, her co-worker's cousin. The couple felt sorry to leave him at the bus station alone in that bad weather. Therefore, they stopped by him and offered him a ride to his home. Atondi was extremely happy and grateful to the couple for such a kind offer. He sat in the back seat with Yosika. Atondi was overwhelmed with joy to seat next to Yosika. It was something he could have never imagined, based on the fact that Bala had turned him down in terms of intimate relationship. Eventually, so much was going on in his mind at that time as he had reported ultimately.

However when they had arrived at his home, suddenly, they noticed that Atondi's cousin Belinda, the school teacher or aunt Mutema's co-worker was at Atondi's home that evening. She was actually waiting eagerly for his cousin Aleyi to get back from school, because she had an urgent message to notify him regarding his father's health status.

As soon as the car stopped in front of Atondi's door, Belinda suddenly, stood up at the threshold in order to take a close look at Atondi who was actually getting out of that car. Surprisingly, she had noticed her co-worker Esperance, seating next to the driver. Thus, she shouted, Esperance! Is that you driving Aleyi home? Where did you find him? Esperance replied that we happened to stop at the University Campus, and waited to pick up our niece Yosika. And, therefore, we saw Aleyi standing at the bus station alone. I actually recognized him as your cousin, so we decided to give him a ride instead of letting him stand there alone in this bad weather. Belinda could not stop thanking Esperance and her husband for their kindness. She then invited them to come inside Aleyi's place for a few minutes. Aleyi was glad that Yosika's aunt and her husband included Yosika had accepted that short invitation of entering in his place. He was somewhat nervous. The guests however, had noticed that Aleyi's home was cozy and neat for a bachelor.

Aleyi and Belinda offered the guests some snacks, Mikate (donut) and Coke-Cola. After spending thirty minutes with them, they departed. That incident was actually a point of contact between Aleyi and Yosika.

EPISODE 3

Yosika's Activities at the University of Kinshasa

In college, as a law major, Yosika met two fellows in the faculty of law, Masamba and Likuta. Both of them were her best classmates. Shortly after one month, Yosika found out that Masamba and Likuta were Atondi's closest friends. Every now and then, Aleyi would ask his friends to stop at his home and do their homework by him, because it was a quiet place. However, Yosika was not aware of this situation until later on.

At the beginning of the semester, Yosika was having a hard time to adjust herself with some college courses. Most of her grades were average. She had been studying alone at her aunt's home. She was striving to improve her grades, but her own efforts appeared not to be successful to increase her grades. However, Masamba and Likuta had always studied together. Yosika had noticed that they always had the highest marks in class. So, she became very curious and wanted to know how is it that they did not encounter the same difficulty that she had been experiencing. Masamba took the lead, and explained to her that the best way to succeed was to study in group of two or three students. The reason for this, Masamba said, was to clarify any ambiguity one might be facing on certain subject. Further, they had offered Bala the opportunity to join them, if she had so desired.

Bala was interested to join them because she wanted to do as well as they did. Further, they had explained to her that it was preferably to meet at their best friend's home, because he lived alone, and his place was convenient to concentrate in their school matters. At first, Yosika had no slightest idea that the friend whom her classmates have been referring to was Aleyi Atondi. She was quite shocked when she finally found out that it was he. She asked her classmates "how long have you actually known this fellow?" She was told that they knew him for quite a while. Likuta clarified that Atondi and he were related by marriage. Further, he explained that his second cousin had married Atondi's second cousin; and for this reason, they had become very close.

Eventually, Yosika was no longer thrilled to join them because she did not feel that it would be appropriate for her to keep on going at Atondi's home. She had been very reluctant to do so at first because Bala was actually embarrassed to face Atondi, due to the unkind words which she had addressed him in the past when he once proposed to her. She felt that the proposal issue had caused him a serious resentment underneath.

However, when she was told at first that the best place they were to meet for study was "their best friend Atondi's home. Instinctively, Bala replied, "Oh, I cannot go there, unfortunately! Massamba and Likuta noticed that Yosika began asking consecutive question. "Does it have to be there? There is no other place to meet?" Bala was actually cynical of that home. Masamba and Likuta told Yosika that, "Meeting at their parents' homes was out of the question, because they came from a large family each one. In addition, there was so much noise around their homes, because the children were always playing, running up and down, and screaming their heads off. Therefore, due to this sort of disruption, we had opted to meet at Atondi's home, because he is a bachelor, and his place is quiet. Therefore it helps us to remain focused.

Her classmates somehow had made several attempts to convince Bala that Aleyi did not disturb them at all. Besides, he was most of the time out of his house, trying to carry out some business activities after the school hours. In fact, by the time he gets back home, we have at that time, completed our projects. Masamba and Likuta assured her that everything works out harmoniously, and that there was no need to be concerned about it."

Obviously, the school works became overwhelming for Bala, and she had also noticed that her academic performance seemed to become very weak, whereas both of her classmates were performing extremely well. Further, she also observed that the instructors spoke highly about them. Masamba and Likuta were referred to as prominent students. Bala as any other students in class contemplated

Masamba and Likuta's aptitude very much. She pondered a while about joining friends at Atondi's home in order to improve her grades. However, she had to actually weigh her pros and cons of taking such an action.

She felt that she had three issues to deal with. The first one was the fact that she had turned Atondi's marriage proposal down. The second one was to deal with her aunts' conservative attitude, how would they actually view her as a female being found in the company of Masamba and Likuta on a regular basis? The third and the most important issue was fear of being dismissed from University due to poor performance, and would she ever face her beloved parents if she winds up failing?

Based on the latest issue, Bala was finally persuaded to go with her classmates at Atondi's place in order to do class projects with them. Her goal was to improve her school performance. She was indeed convinced that studying alone at her aunt's home would not stop her from failing and being dismissed from School. She therefore, decided to join Masamba and Likuta.

Eventually, things happened exactly in the manner in which her classmates had described at Aleyi's home. Atondi had never bothered her, besides from saying "hello Yosika, and also asking her about her aunt Mutema and aunt Lesa welfare."

Since she begun to study, and work together with both of her classmates, Bala noticed that her grades began improving gradually. She felt very comfortable to continue doing her projects with those two fellows. On one hand, Atondi was so embarrassed, and he did not have the back bone to reveal to his friends that Yosika had turned him down. He had kept that secret for himself. On the other hand, Bala felt awkward to tell her classmates about her incident with Aleyi as well. However, Atondi and Yosika knew what had happened in the past between them. Technically, each of them was still wondering whether or not one of them had actually revealed that incident to either Masamba or Likuta. Apparently, there had been no sign showing such thing.

While she was busy with her school activities, spending time with her classmates at Atondi's home, her aunt Esperance and her husband began to wonder why Bala was coming back home so late from school. Bala on the other hand, knew perfectly well that she ought them a clear explanation about her after school schedule. However, she failed to do so because she had thought telling them the truth would make the matter worse.

EPISODE 4

Communication Gap Between Yosika and Her Aunts

Because Bala was afraid to confess that she actually was spending time studying with her classmates at Aleyi Atondi's home, she chose to give excuses which appeared to be invalid unfortunately to her relatives.

Therefore, every time her aunt Esperance would ask her to give them a good reason why she was returning home so late, Yosika would make up an inappropriate excuse. She would reply, "I actually stopped at aunt Lesa's home." This situation went on for quite a while. Bala would sometimes, indeed, stay at aunt Lesa's place, but this was on a rare occasion. It was another way around, on the days which Bala would spend few days at her aunt Lesa's place, she actually would use aunt Mutema's home as an excuse of returning home late. Bala had thought that having two different homes, would actually justify her returning home late. The situation had gotten confused somehow. Intuitively, however, both of her aunts started to suspect that Yosika must have been doing something wrong. When in reality, Yosika was innocent. She did nothing, but study.

Eventually, Yosika started to feel that she was being put under pressure from both of her aunts. She knew that she was not being abused by either one of her classmates or even by Atondi. Unfortunately, no one could possibly believe her. They were actually projecting a negative outcome. When aunt Mutema's neighbors heard the complaints about Bala' s behavior, they too, started being so noisy, and started to get involved in Bala's issues. The same situation happened around her aunt Lesa's home. Neighbors also heard the complaints, and they too began to keep an eye on Yosika's move. It was a strange issue; only God alone could actually confirm that Yosika Bala was above all that unnecessary suspicious. On several occasions however, neighbors would confirm, seeing Yosika walking with two men, and that was on a regular basis. Technically, Yosika had indeed the habit of walking with those gentlemen, but they were just her classmates. Unfortunately, neighbors viewed things negatively, especially the fact that they had always seen her coming in and out Aleyi's home.

Sometimes, however, Aleyi escorted them at the bus station. On that particular day, however, aunt Mutema's neighbor happened to be around Atondi area. And therefore, he had perceived Bala indeed coming out of Atondi's place along with three other men following behind her. The neighbor's eyes were wide open to notice those three gentlemen accompanied by one single female. The neighbor, who had been made aware of Yosika issues, could hardly wait to reach the Yosika Bala's aunt home. He was eager to report the incident without missing a slightest detail. He stated which borough he had been that day, and how he spotted Yosika, coming out of that house; he made sure to stress on the fact that she was the only female followed by three men behind her. That kind of a report was enough to get aunt Mutema and her husband furious with their niece.

When her aunt questioned Yosika concerning that allegation, upon her arrival home, and she, not knowing that the neighbor had already betrayed her, she unfortunately, utilized her usual excuse. She replied, "Well, I came late because I had stopped at aunt Lesa's place. Yosika was not aware that a neighbor had actually spotted her coming from Atondi's place along with three men. This situation created a confirmation that Yosika had been involved in some unpleasant relationship.

Yosika invalid excuses made aunt Esperance very furious, and then her aunt said to her, "Just because you have not been truthful all this time either to me or to your aunt Lesa, I am hitting you today for the first time; and then, I will report this incident to your parents. Bala's parents were living in Bukavu city at that time. Bala was actually bitten unfairly. Because of that unfair treatment, she decided to depart from aunt Esperance's place and moved to her aunt Lesa's home. She had stayed there for six months without returning back to her aunt Mutema's home. She resented her for that period of time.

While she was living at aunt Lesa, the same situation reappeared. She did not want to fail the course, and therefore she continued to study with her classmates again, and it was at Aleyi's home as usual. Yosika continued to be frightened in revealing her study schedule with her classmates at Atondi's home to her aunt. She could not have done it because she was aware that her aunt was very conservative; and no matter what she would have said to her, and whichever manner she would have presented the situation, her aunts would have interpreted, and viewed the whole scene absolutely wrong. Further, aunt Lesa's mind would be going wild, picturing her niece coming out with three men! Naturally, aunt Lesa would have viewed this picture as being absurd.

This actually was the reason why Bala had preferred to come out with excuses rather than telling either one of her aunts the truth. Regardless to her personal judgment, things still turned out completely on the negative side for the rest of her life. And then, Yosika recalled the preaching of his grandfather, on the book of

> *Job 3:25 – for the thing which I greatly feared is come upon me, and that which was afraid of is come unto me.*

In fact, Yosika was not lucky enough, while she was staying at her aunt Lesa, a male neighbor had actually seen her walking together with three gentlemen (Masamba, Likuta and Atondi). Bala was the only female among all those three men. Further, the male neighbor was one of the noisiest people around that neighborhood. Therefore, he made Bala's issue as if it were his own. So, he had immediately stopped at Ms. Lesa Bala's home that same evening in order to report that so called incident. That man had made such an awful remark about Yosika. Upon hearing that unpleasant remark, aunt Lesa obviously became very upset. Then, as soon as Yosika had walked in the house, aunt Lesa called her, saying, "Yosika, now you come here!" Yosika wondered now what seems to be the matter. Aunt Lesa continued, "Listen to me, and if you are going to start with this kind of indecent life, surrounded by men at all time, you will never complete your college education or even get married to a nobleman.

She continued, saying, "Remember a good man nowadays prefers to marry a well educated woman. Right after the downfall of the African civilization, the school education for women was never regarded as any marriage issue, to our great grandparents.

That is the plain truth. However, women today, are not as those of my great grandparents' time. During that period of time, women were not obligatory to pursuit their school education. It was not required because they were just occupied with house chores. Currently, however, educated Congolese women are in demand. Nowadays, some women are actually running very important offices, and holding positions of Trust! Child, you must keep up with all the necessary innovations or else you will be relapsed into bad habit. In addition be aware that nobody would want to associate with a person who has some undesirable attributes.

Years ago, aunt Lesa continued, people viewed things differently when a baby boy was born. The father used to be overwhelmed with joy, because the boy was considered to be a backbone of the family, whereas the baby girl brought a discouragement to her father, because a girl's role was somewhat limited in the family. She was only good to get married and produce children. Ultimately, she would then continue with routine chores. Therefore, women's education was unessential during that time. That belief is now obsolete. Currently, parents are being illumined, because they viewing innovations in every country, as well as in every gender. The illumination in people's mind is actually a God's gift to the world. It is an indication that the Lord is really returning very soon.

Therefore, parents could care less at this point in time, whether they give birth to a baby boy or to a baby girl, because the gender is no longer a barrier to women. Aunt Lesa continued, Yosika, your parents are illumined. They know about all these changes. This is actually the reason why, they sent you here. They would like you to be evolved. University will open you the door to many opportunities. Aunt Lesa Bala repeated, you are here actually to acquire a higher level of education, Yosika.

Why do you really want to ruin your life? Why are you being seen always surrounded by two or sometimes three men? Not once, but on a regular basis! Yosika, can't you find females friends?" She reprimanded her repeatedly, saying, Yosika, didn't your mother educate you that theoretically, men must hang out with men and female must also hang out with female?"

Aunt Lesa rested a while, and then, she resumed, Yosika, if your mother was unable to bring these things to your attention, well I, as your father's sister must do it. Remember, officially, men stick with men, because they have common things to talk about. So, are women, their conversation and experience in life are quite different from men's. It is indeed illogical for a female to neglect her own gender and jump to another. What have you got in common with those gentlemen, Yosika?" She asked, staring at her.

Aunt Lesa couldn't stop to remind her niece the real reason why she found herself in that city. She continued again, "Darling, remember, your parents sent you here in Kinshasa to study, and not to be a street girl. What are you really looking for? Your parents are well to do, and they spend lot of money on you. Why are you wasting your time with those fellows who have nothing to offer you?" She said. Certainly, Yosika did not know where to begin explaining that whole situation which was actually far from her aunts' ideology. Yosika felt helpless, could not find a suitable word that could calm her aunt's anxiety. She had noticed that, Lesa Bala appeared very depressed.

Yosika made an attempt to give her aunt a clue about what was really going on between those so called three men and her. Aunt Lesa would not give her a chance to speak..

Aunt Lesa went on, "Yosika if you feel that you are no longer interested in pursuing your education, and that you prefer rather to get married after high school, well in that case, you should find a well to do man. Child, do not fool yourself about marriage, aunt Lesa stressed that fact to Yosika. She said to her that "Marriage is a very serious commitment." Let whoever man you choose to marry you, meets the dowry obligations, on both father as well as mother's side. After the traditional ceremony, we also will require a church wedding in order to seal that marriage. The Christian marriage must be built on a rock for it to survive, and we in our family believe that God is our Rock," She concluded.

Yosika got very upset and started to cry, and said to her aunt: "Aunt Lesa, believe me those fellows are just my classmates. There is nothing happening in terms of intimacy." Aunt Lesa, replied "Do not lie to me, Yosika. Many people are confirming about your behavior. I think you should return to your aunt Esperance's home, if you are going to continue telling me deceitful things. I can no longer cop with this awful behavior of yours. Obviously, you are embarrassing me as well as the entire family. Remember that even our Pastor has been made aware of this awful situation. Which Pastor would ever like to conduct a wedding ceremony of a young lady who actually has a bad testimony? I actually would not think of any, she said to her", shaking her head.

Yosika was really disturbed with all this false accusations. She had no other relative in the entire city where she could have moved in temporarily until she could she was able to reach her parents, who lived far away from the city capital.

She had realized that both of her aunts had actually lost trust in her. However, at the same time Bala did not want to fail in college. She had noticed that studying with those classmates was quite beneficial and informative for her, because her grades had improved immensely during that period of time. Bala also had noticed that the school projects became very intense and the courses were getting harder. She had indeed realized that studying alone could not have helped her college performance. Consequently, she was willing to continue taking that risk. Yosika found herself as though she was between the devil and the deep sea.

Considering the fact that in the following weeks, she had few tests scheduled, Bala was determined to pass all of them. And therefore, prior to meeting her friends at their usual place of study, she took her school books as well as some of personal belongings. At the end of her study session with her friends, she decided to go back to her Aunt Esperance Mutema's home. After six months, Yosika's anger against her aunt Esperance had been lessened. The harsh words had been faded away from her mind during that time. The study session was short that day, because it was just a matter of reviewing of a very few topics. So she had arrived at her aunt earlier than customary, that evening. Aunt Esperance was already made aware of the fact that aunt Lesa on the other hand, had also reprimanded Yosika for her so called late schedule. Therefore, as soon as Yosika had arrived at aunt Esperance's home, her aunt was so impulsive. She started to scream at her spontaneously, saying, "Yosika what seems to be wrong with you? Wherever you go, you are actually bringing nothing but trouble.

Lesa will not put up with your nonsense, neither will I", she said to her, and she continued, "but I would like you to remember that I still maintain my words as well as my position; and if you are not listening to either one of us, then, I will not let you come back in my house either." Yosika stood by her aunt's doorway immovable for about fifteen minutes, and holding her school bag and some of her personal items.

Shortly after that, her aunt closed her door without giving her access. Bala waited for a few minutes to see whether or not her aunt would change her mind, and hopefully to let her in. It did not happen, unfortunately. Yosika was puzzled, and did not know where to go. Aunt Lesa did not want her back in her house. Aunt Esperance was even worse. Both of them thought of Yosika as being an insubordinate niece. Their egos were eventually hurt, and they couldn't continue to deal with a "rebellious" niece, so they thought. Yosika was somewhat confused that evening. She couldn't go either to Masamba or Likuta's homes to seek a refuge, because they came from a huge family. She also knew that it was useless to actually do so, because she had never been introduced to their families. Bala felt that taking that approach would definitely seem bizarre. She was actually left with one last and ugly choice in mind; and that awful choice was Atondi's home. Apparently, it was a tough decision for her to make. She wondered what in the world would anyone think of me, Yasoki, going to Aleyi's house in the evening such as this one. She thought that taking that kind of approach would be out of the ordinary as well. Bala sensed that even Atondi would find it peculiar, but probably he wouldn't mind.

Deep down in her heart, however, she was still afraid of her aunts' reaction. She was absolutely certain that if her aunts would find out that she has gone to Aleyi's place, they would make their hypothesis becomes a reality. Therefore, any explanation regarding this situation would sound as though I am actually attempting to rationalize the situation. It would therefore be in vain.

Regardless, Yosika took the bus from the borough of the "City Salongo" where her aunt Esperance was residing, then went to the borough of "Lemba" where Aleyi

Atondi was living. She actually felt humiliated to take that direction. Bala's sincere intention had been of asking Atondi to allow her to say at his place for a very short duration while she was making an attempt to reach her parents in Bakavu or Kivu Province and ask for assistance.

EPISODE 5

Yosika Chooses the Last and Wrong Alternative

Atondi was really surprised to see Yosika at that late hour. It was after the study session had ended. At first, he thought that she probably came back to see whether or not she had forgotten an important item in his house. He found out however that it was a serious dilemma. Atondi noticed that Bala appeared very depressed. Prior to letting her in his house, Atondi stood at the threshold and questioned her, "What seems to be the matter Yosika? She answered that Aleyi, I am actually facing a serious problem, and I need to speak with you. Hearing those words, Atondi decided to let her in immediately.

Bala continued, while she was still standing, "You are not going to believe how human beings could actually rationalize things. Would you believe that both of my aunts do not believe that Masamba and Likuta are nothing but my classmates, and that we come here just to study in group so that I too can maintain better grades?

It is appalling to experience such negative feelings coming from both of my aunts about me. Atondi said, "I actually do not see any reason why they should be angry at you for that reason." Yosika, replied, the reason is just because I have been returning later than the time they expect me to arrive. Both of them have actually put me out of their homes, as of today. My parents are in Bukavu, as I had previously mentioned to you. It is going to take at least a week prior to reaching them. As it stands now, I really have no place to go. Atondi asked her, "Even your aunt Lesa Bala, who appeared to be so understanding and patient, put you out as well?" Yes, even her too, she replied.

Apparently, they have wrong assumptions about me. They actually think that "I am defiant", it is just because I have been returning late after the school hours. Basically, I do not know whether it is my fault, because I have not really confessed that I come to study at your place with friends. The reason I avoided telling them the truth about my after school schedule, is due to the fact that they view things differently. They are very conservative individuals, and based on their perspective, they would stop me from studying with my classmates. I do not actually wish to fail, and this is why I have been taking all these risks.

Atondi understood that Yosika was really facing a dilemma. There was a high degree of confusions between her relatives and herself. She appeared worn out completely. So, he attempted to console her afterwards. Atondi did not have any cooked food at that time to offer Yosika that evening. However, on her way, Yosika had considered it, and purchased a loaf of bread and three medium size fried fish, termed, "Thompson". She also had bought two bottles of orange drink. Atondi gave her a plate to place her food. She ate some and shared some with Atondi. The leftover was conserved in Atondi's small freeze.

Shortly after that, Atondi had begun to speak with her positively about that confusion. He told her that, "I believe that your aunts do not mean any harm to you. I think they are just attempting to be protective of you. Unfortunately, they are jumping into a wrong conclusion," he concluded. Atondi asked Yosika, "Have you tried to explain, in detail, your daily schedule to your aunts? Yosika replied, "I may actually explain thousand times to both of my aunts, in the attempt to convince them that my relationship with my classmates is based solely on the fact that they are helping me with my school work. I am actually the one who needs their help and not another way around. And therefore, I am just striving to perform well in School. Regardless to how much I can attempt to explain, they still will not believe me and that where the dilemma is coming from.

Aleyi encouraged her, saying that is exactly what you should actually tell your aunts. Yosika, replied, but they are on a defensive side. They just would not give me a chance to communicate with them clearly.

Apparently, their hypothesis has become a reality. It is pathetic Atondi said. I can understand both sides.

Obviously, this is nothing but confusions according to my standpoint.

Atondi asked Yosika, "Have you actually tried to explain to your aunts everything about this whole situation?" Miss Bala answered that, "Aleyi, as I have just explained; I had wanted to explain to them thoroughly, however, I refrained doing so, because my aunts do not let me communicate with them freely." Their mind appears to jumps just like a monkey does, from one branch to another.

Atondi asked Yosika the permission to relate this issue to his cousin Belinda, who was aunt's Esperance co-worker. Yosika therefore allowed him to do so. Atondi took the opportunity to narrate the entire situation to her cousin Belinda. His goal was to make his cousin Belinda, Yakima's advocate, and present the issue in a different angle.

Miss Belinda, Atondi's cousin was receptive enough and decided to explain the matter to both of her aunts. They appeared to comprehend partially, but were still skeptical with Yosika, nevertheless. This incident had permitted Atondi to resume his marriage proposal to Yosika. He seized the opportunity. She had no alternative at that time, due to such circumstance. And therefore, she gave her consent under that pressure. Atondi and his cousin Belinda went to Yosika's aunts to tell them that Yosika and Aleyi were planning to get married. Aunt Esperance shouted! "No way, Belinda, Yosika's parents will never accept that kind of relationship which lacks any solid background.

She continued Yosika's parents actually have a very high expectation of their daughter. Belinda, Esperance said, "Please, tell your cousin Aleyi, right now, not to dare making any attempt to influence my niece in that kind of relationship. I assure you, it would be a nightmare to our family," Mutema told her co-worker those types of harsh words without any reservation. Finally, Mutema turned to both Aleyi and Yosika who stood in close proximity, and said that, "You two cannot be husband and wife by all means. Aleyi, you will never be able to support a child who is born in such a high class family!"

Yosika, who had been hurt emotionally, responded angrily to her aunt, "Yes" I am going to marry Aleyi anyhow." Atondi has always had the impression that Esperance Mutema had never liked him from the beginning.

Belinda had tried to talk Aleyi out of that relationship with Yosika. She advised him that customarily, before you marry a woman, you must get her parents and her entire family's consent. You do not jump to marriage without honoring the preliminary steps. She added, "It is very dangerous to marry a woman against her family's will, because marriage is a very big commitment.

Belinda continued, did you actually hear the manner in which Esperance had spoken about this girl's family? At the present time, you are still in school. You do not have any decent job or income. That is already an indication that it would be impossible for you to support this young lady. In addition, she said to him, "Your father in the village is not well, his health is deteriorating daily. At the present time, I would wish you to concentrate on your father's welfare.

Besides, nobody in our family would be able to assist you with the dowry expense." Belinda, insisted, "Aleyi, I would advise you, please leave this girl alone. Please do not get involved with her in order to prevent further problems." In addition, Belinda said, Aleyi, I actually had told you everything that I think which you should know regarding your involvement with this young lady. However, if you choose to be disobedient, well in that case, I would not want to get involved any further in this matter.

Atondi actually agreed with Belinda that Congolese culture requires the consent of both families prior to taking any kind of preliminary steps pertaining to the engagement.

EPISODE 6

Atondi Meets Luzola, Yosika's Uncle in Her Native Village

Considering the fact that Yosika's parents resided extremely far from the Capital city and besides, the plane ticket was very costly for Atondi's income. In addition, he had never travelled by air since he was born. He figured the opportunity to marry Yosika was at hand, and he wanted to seize it without fail. And therefore, he decided to travel by truck owned by a well known businessman located nearby Yosika's village. That outstanding businessman had been educated by Yosika's grandfather, who was a retired pastor at that time. This businessman had developed a lot of consideration for anyone related to Yosika's grandfather. He would speak highly about him.

In fact, Yosika's grandfather had been a great teacher to all of his students, especially to that businessman. The man himself repeatedly confirmed this fact to many people. The fare to actually go to Yosika's native area, by truck cost Atondi close to nothing. S, he decided to go to Yosika's village in order to meet Yosika's uncle. In his way, he had purchased one bottle of a palm drink, a traditional wine. According to the culture, this bottle of wine is designated to present it to the fiancée's uncle as a symbol or a sign of pre-dowry. Atondi could have bought more than one bottle of palm wine, but he could not afford it. Yosika's uncle was young, he was about the same age with Aleyi, but was very successful. His name was Luzola. He had received his mechanic training in Kinshasa, the capital city of the country, and had acquired an extensive experience in this field while he was in Kinshasa.

Luzola decided to establish his small shop in the farm which he had inherited from his matriarchal uncle. Apparently, his mechanic skills were well sought by many truck drivers, who had formed the habits of traveling from Kinshasa to Lozola's area for trading purpose. Luzola was well organized in terms of making auto repair. In addition, he travelled frequently to Germany in order to buy trucks and other automobiles parts. Aleyi had noticed that Luzola also had five mechanic assistants. They were very polite, and they always addressed him with a lot of respect, "Patron" or Boss, whenever they approached the boss for assistance.

When Aleyi Atondi arrived in Luzola's home, he was quite impressed to see such an organization. He had first noticed several trucks and different vehicles lined up on the street, close to that Property. All of them were actually waiting to be repaired. Besides from that, the farmer had a big modern brick house. The house had six big bed rooms.

The action speaks louder than words. Atondi then realized that indeed Yosika came from a well to do family. Upon noticing all those things, Atondi then developed an inferiority complex because in his village, Yosika would have never encountered such a high class image. His family was very poor in his village, and they lived in a small house.

While he was observing all those things and comparing with his own background, Aleyi started to recall everything which Yosika's aunt, Esperance Mutema had voiced regarding Atondi's attempts to marry Yosika. He figured, if Yosika's uncle could have this kind of high class life while he is residing in the village, then he wondered how Yosika's parents' home might look like in Bukavu city. He was somewhat nervous to introduce himself at first, and to actually voice the reason for which his visit entailed.

Furthermore, Atondi was very embarrassed because he only had one bottle of palm wine to present to Yosika's uncle, and to make the situation worse, he came alone with no other family member to accompany him or to witness the event. Nevertheless, he was well received somehow. Based on the culture, Luzola was quite aware that the one bottle of wine presented on that initial step did not guarantee or indicate the consent of marriage. So, Luzola had asked Atondi whether or not he had spoken to Bala's parents in Bukavu regarding this matter? Atondi's answered, "Well not yet, but I will, as soon as I get back to Kinshasa." Upon presenting his pre-dowry bottle of traditional wine, he made a promise to return for the real and serious ceremony in the near future after the completion of his study which would lead him to acquire a better employment at that time, he thought. This promised was never fulfilled, unfortunately.

As soon as Atondi had returned from Yosika's village, Atondi and Miss Bala amazingly, claimed themselves a married couple. However, there had never been any sort of marriage ceremony, whether traditional, church or even from the "Commune" (City Hall). Yosika gave her consent because of the pressure she had been experiencing from both of her aunts. Obviously, that relationship was never based on genuine love on Bala's standpoint. However, Atondi was naïve. He sincerely believed that it was based on sincere love.

The most peculiar thing in this whole scenario was the fact that no one had had the audacity of notifying Yosika's parents about such confused circumstances on time. They probably would have intervened, and prevent undesirable consequences. As far as Atondi was concerned however, he had married Yosika based on that one bottle of palm wine which he had offered Yosika's uncle in the village. So, they began living as husband and wife from that time on. Shortly, afterwards, Yosika conceived and had a baby boy. Unfortunately, she was obligated to discontinue her college education, which had been the main goal of her life. Naturally, it was a heartbreaking experience for Yosika. Atondi however completed his education, and detained his bachelors' degree in Finance.

Aunt Esperance could not stand Aleyi Atondi because he did not have sufficient income to take care of her niece Yosika, who came from a well to do family. Aunt Lesa was slightly tolerant of Atondi, but to some degree, she was somewhat sad as well, because she and her entire family had a very high expectancy of Yosika. They had wished her to pursuit her college education and receive high achievement in life.

EPISODE 7

THE BEGINNING of ATONDI'S DILEMMA

As soon as Atondi graduated, his country, the Congo, RDC and its governmental system began to deteriorate rapidly. It became extremely difficult for anyone to find an entry level position either in the Finance department or any other sectors. The corruption became obvious in every sector. Atondi could not find a job in his field of study. Eight months later, Yosika conceived again. Life became awfully difficult for Yosika who had come from a well to do family. Atondi's minor income from his small business was actually meaningless. It began to decrease extensively, and could hardly make the ends meet. Evidently, Yosika and her son were experiencing a high degree of malnutrition. Both of her aunts started to become very frustrated with Atondi, especially the fact that he got Yosika pregnant again, so soon, and without realizing that he had been incapable to nourish the first child as well as his wife. Apparently, everyone was concerned, and wondered how in the world he was going to manage that subtle situation.

As it was previously mentioned, Aunt Lesa Bala was a widow, and she had just enough money to support herself and her daughter. Aunt Esperance Mutema, on the other hand, however, had a sufficient income because her husband was a journalist and she was a high school teacher. In addition, they had some private business on a side. Esperance was too close to her big sister, Yosika's mother. As far as aunt Mutema was concerned, Yosika was treated as though she had been her own daughter.

Aunt Mutema was very spiritual and courageous as well. Regardless to her frustration towards her niece, for having made such an unwise choice, Esperance had somehow a high degree of compassion. Therefore, she felt obligated to help Yosika and her son devotedly. Her faith in God was so great. She had formed the habit of meditating on the topic of forgiveness as the Lord Jesus had taught the world. She often referred to the following book of the Bible: Matthew 18: 22 Jesus said to him, ""I don't tell you until seven times, but, until seventy times seven. Esperance reminded herself that the Lord had told me to forgive one offense for seventy times seven. That is actually four hundred ninety times. Ma niece Yosika had just made this one big mistake. If I am indeed a child of God, why can't I forgive her from the bottom of my heart? She talks to herself.

Finally, Yosika had felt the heat of marrying a man that could not afford to support his family. She had no other choice except to begin spending time at her aunt Mutema with a child. Aunt Mutema started welcoming her again at her home in order to care for her and her son, because she was afraid of losing her niece and as well as her child. Apparently, Yosika had lost a lot of weight and appeared faded in the eyes of her aunts as well as those of the outsiders who used to admire her beauty. Both of her aunts were very disturbed by that view. In addition, Yosika's second pregnancy had caused her a lot of discomfort.

Aunt Esperance had to keep an eye on her niece's health because she did not want anything to happen to her. Atondi on the other hand, did not have any money to bring his wife to a qualified medical doctor for consultations. Aunt Mutema took control of her niece. She therefore, found her a good gynecologist/obstetrician, who could follow her up very closely, and on a regular basis. That Specialist had outstanding credentials. He had studied in Switzerland, then in the United States of America.

Regardless to aunt Mutema's generosity, Atondi had proven to be an ungrateful person. Due to his inability to cope with serious matters, Atondi developed animosity against aunt Esperance. He was so arrogant and spoke to her disrespectfully, instead being so thankful. Nevertheless, Mutema was so devoted to his wife as well as to his son. Mutema was so spiritual that she adopted another attitude of dealing with him. She actually ignored him completely because she viewed Atondi's behaviors as being childish, and they were lack of refinement.

However, she forgave him and continued to pray for him. Apparently, she and everyone else realized that Atondi was actually feeling guilty and ashamed of himself for having taken the stand of influencing Yosika. Everyone had realized that, based on Yosika appearance, if she wound up marrying him, it must have been through Atondi's adulations; otherwise, she would have never given him her consent. Besides, people knew that that relationship was never founded on any sort of official ceremony.

Based on her spiritual attributes, aunt Mutema did what needed to be done at that time, in order to care and protect her niece as well as her child, without feeling any intimidation. Although aunt Mutema had put Yosika under the care of a very competent and reputable gynecologist/obstetrician, when the labor days were approaching, Atondi brought Yosika to a certain family doctor whose practice was unknown to many women.

Besides, his office was located in an indecent borough. Yosika reported the incident to her aunt, saying that Atondi, said, "To hell with your aunt's doctor. Esperance actually wants to show off. In addition, he added that, that Specialist is extremely expensive. He just refuses for me to go give birth over there. Further, he said that if your aunt gives you money in order to go and see that Specialist, make sure that you bring that money to me, because it is needed to buy food here in this house." Atondi became very imposing. Yosika realized it, because the fellow started to speak to her without any consideration

She actually noticed his harsh language for the first time, on the day that she wanted to throw a small broken chair away. Atondi was furious that day, and he shouted at Yosika, "Put that little chair back where it stood. Yosika tried to explain that both legs are broken on that little chair. I think it would be preferable that we put it out in order to prevent any accident to occur. Atondi was fuming to hear such an invalid explanation, and out of his state of anger, he told Yosika, "From your parents' house, how many chairs have you brought here in this house?" He added, "What did your mother gave you? Atondi's statements were too strong for Yosika to digest. However, she chose not to comment. Ultimately, the entire family had heard it, and Atondi had to face the reality of his life.

After learning Atondi's concerns about the Specialist that Esperance Mutema had selected in order to better care for Yosika, Mutema brought Yosika to aunt Lesa's place. Both of them discussed the matter thoroughly, and then, they decided to let Yosika stay by her aunt Mutema during those few days. Apparently Yosika had begun experiencing some labor symptoms at that time.

They knew that Atondi was incompetent to handle such a delicate situation. Therefore, they had decided not to take any chances. Her doctor on the other hand, had exemplified his medical abilities, and he was actually following her up very closely, until the following day when the patient gave birth to another healthy baby boy.

The second boy was actually born when the first child was almost nine months. The responsibility of supporting two children and a wife was just overwhelming for Atondi. Aunt Mutema and her husband did everything they could for Yosika and both of her sons, while her parents were still stationed in Bukavu city. Esperance devoted to help her niece for her sister's sake, Yosika's mother. Both sisters, have always been very close to each other. That was the manner in which their beloved parents had actually trained them. They had to look after each other. They were not to place money before the love of God and the love of their family. Furthermore, they were trained that they should always remember that based on their culture, children go to the mother's side because they practiced matriarchal system.

During that time, Esperance Mutema started to recall every piece of advice which she had received from her parents during her childhood education. The recollection of her mother's voice, sounded so strongly in her mind. She repeatedly, remembered the following words from her mother's mouth, "Beloved children, you shall love each other more than you would love anything else in your life. Further, you shall never put money before the love of your sister or your brother. In addition, don't you ever forget that if you should lose anything regardless of its value, including money, you may always replace it by the grace of God.

All of us should know that everything belongs to the Creator. However, if you neglect your sister or your brother, just because you have acquired some material thing, and then you begin to feel as though you are sprouting wings to fly, you will wind up regretting it for eternity. So, children, remember that once you lose your sister or your brother that would actually be it! You would never replace her or him again!" Recovery is only meant for the items of this world, and never for life. Life is precious, whether it is yours or your brothers or sisters. You shall always remember to preserve life as long as you shall live, including the lives of every human beings," said their mother.

Aunt Mutema had always had a compassion attitude towards her niece. However, she became frustrated due to the fact that her niece had actually interrupted her higher education. This error was due to the fact of having listened to Atondi's adulations. Her main concern about the whole situation was the fact that the man was irresponsible to provide for his family. In addition, he appeared to be less attractive for her beautiful niece. Fortunately, both sons were extremely handsome. They were the really picture of Yosika, and none of them took after Atondi. Everyone was actually relieved for that fact.

At first, aunt Mutema did not know that aunt Lesa had informed Yosika's parents regarding their daughter's adventure with Atondi; although, she had done it at the later stage. As far as she was concerned, Yosika's father had a hot temper, and therefore, she had preferred to communicate with them gradually in order to prevent any negative reaction between parents and their daughter.

Unfortunately, aunt Lesa had already made them aware about the unpleasant situation that had already occurred. Naturally, they were disappointed to learn about their daughter's unwise action and choice. Based on their comments, they were not eager to speak with her again. Considering Yosika's father's temper, Esperance knew that the niece would not get any more help from her parents. She actually arranged her own work schedule. This was in the attempt to permit her niece to attain a training school while she would be watching her children.

Regardless to her outspoken attitude which Atondi hated so much, Esperance had exemplified her spiritual virtues. She forgave her niece completely. Yosika had also asked for forgiveness for her defiance to both of her aunts. Furthermore, she had confessed the motive that was behind such unwise approach which had worsened her aspiration. Obviously, it was too late to remedy the damage, and of course, she had to bear the consequences of her unwise decision.

EPISODE 8

Aunt Mutema Sent Yosika To a Beauty School

Esperance however, wanted Yosika to acquire a skill which could help her to become self-sufficient in the future. Therefore, she took the responsibility of sending her to the nearby Beauty School in order to receive one year training; so that she could become a hair dresser. That particular school belonged to a Congolese-Haitian couple. The tuition was expensive and the final exam was actually broken into several different sessions. Students began to whine for that fact.

The graduation date kept on changing just in the attempt to extend the school session, and collect additional tuition, spitefully. It was also noticed that each area of practice was being lengthened, and required additional fees which amounted to two year school tuition. Aunt Mutema was determined, however, to continuing financing the training until its completion.

Apparently, Yosika was a role model in school. Her instructors spoke highly about her ability to master her skills. In addition, volunteer customers who came to have their hair done at that School had always preferred to have their heir done by Yosika. She was in demand because she had a special flair which no other student had. Further, her sophistication and personality made everyone like her. Due to all those attributes, Yosika was always being invited to dress up brides whenever there was a wedding ceremony around the city. She was always being referred to different wealthy clients, who offered a moderate amount of money in tips. Aunt Esperance was so grateful to God for allowing her to become an instrument of promoting her niece instead of letting her mind vegetates. Mutema had just refused to perceive Yosika as a faded housewife. She knew somehow that she could explore some other qualities in her even though she was no longer going to become a lawyer as she had initially planned. She did not believe that because she had interrupted her college education, Yosika could not develop different skills. Esperance had faith in her niece. Yosika was so grateful for the chance which her aunt had given her.

Although most of the people had actually thought that she was no longer good for anything else, except to wind up as a miserable housewife. Further, some individuals had begun to mock Yosika. They projected all sort of negative images toward Yosika such as, She will wind up breast feeding children for the rest of her life," because Atondi made her appeared worn out and faded like a dead flower. Fortunately, Esperance Mutema stood against that view.

Then, nine months later, Yosika and her aunts received good news from Yosika's parents. They were moving from Bukavu city to Kinshasa. Aunt Lesa Bala was overwhelmed with joy because that would actually be the first time, she and her brother would actually have the opportunity of living in the same city. She was extremely happy for the fact that she and her brother will be seeing each other on a regular basis. Evidently, since Lesa Bala and her brother had been married to their spouses, they hardly saw each other. Occasionally, however, they would get together for a very short duration, and that was once every two or three years.

When Yosika's parents had arrived in Kinshasa, Atondi had almost two months of the unpaid rents. He could not give any positive impression to his in-laws. At that time, his landlord was furious and he evicted the couple actually two days after the arrival of Yosika's parents. Fortunately, her parents had a big family house which they had built few years ago in Kinshasa. The house included, five bed rooms and a wide living room and all the comfort. Yosika had come from the family of six children which was composed of four boys and two girls. Her two big brothers and one sister were studying abroad, whereas two young brothers of the age of ten and twelve were still living with her parents. Yosika left her young brothers with her parents when she came to pursuit her education at the University of Kinshasa in the faculty of law.

The day her parents arrived, Yosika was afraid to approach them because of her involvement with a man who was incapable to provide for his children.

However, aunt Esperance had to go with her in order to greet them, because she knew that Yosika's parents were annoyed with their daughter. Upon arrival, Esperance advised Yosika's parents that they actually must learn how to forgive their daughter's mistakes, and love their grandsons with all their hearts; because they were actually innocent creatures. She referred to the Holy Bible, and reminded them to view Yosika a prodigal son. She asked them to recall the reaction of his father when he returned home, subsequently. The word of God indeed has a soothing effect to any Christian who faces a crisis.

Atondi also was nervous to meet Yosika's parents because he knew naturally that they were well to do, and would definitely be very disappointed for the fact that their daughter had not gotten involved with a man of their rank who could have provided her with a high living standard.

However, as soon as Yosika's parents perceived her two sons, they became excited to meet their grandsons. The children resembled their mother completely. Mrs. Bala could not help shouting, "This is a real picture of Yosika! There was absolutely no sign of Atondi in them. They were glad for that view, and they embraced them wholeheartedly.

They also had noticed that Yosika's children were more attached to Esperance Mutema than to their own mother and especially less to their father. They concluded that indeed aunt Esperance had been on top of the whole situation, and offered them unconditional love. Evidently Yosika's mother was so grateful to the child education which her mother imbedded in her mind. Her sister Mutema had actually exemplified it.

EPISODE 9

Atondi Receive Eviction and Moved in His in-Laws' Home

The day which they received the eviction, Yosika joined the children at aunt Mutema's home. She took her luggage and her personal belongings. Atondi on the other hand, was busy trying to take out his most important belongings. He attempted to stack them outside of the apartment. However, he did not have any place to store those items. The landlord felt obligated to seize some of his entertainment devices and other valuable items. Further, Atondi's cousin had told him up front that she regrets to view the predicament he was in however; she had no vacant room at her place to accommodate him and his family, unfortunately.

While Yosika and her two sons were at her aunt Esperance's home, all of a sudden, one of Yosika brothers called in order to inquire about his parents' whereabouts. Right away, aunt Mutema told him that Yosika was standing right next to her. Then she added, unfortunately, her husband Atondi had just received an eviction from his landlord. She also informed him that their parents were staying at the borough of Salongo, in their own house which they had rented to one of the UN agent, while they have been away. The tenants, she continued, were already prepared to move out, and everything pertaining to moving in and out was done harmoniously.

Yosika's brother asked to speak with her sister. His first reaction naturally was, to reprimand her, and saying, "Yosika, now you believe that in life you do not act so quickly, and especially not when you are angry; and in such a confused state of mind!

That is because a good decision must be made with your sound mind, and not when you are irritated. All the wise people will actually confirm my statement." Yosika was nervous because she knew that her entire family has been disturbed by her unpleasant relationship with Atondi. Further, her brother added, "Yosika, now do you understand that Atondi was not a man for you to get involved with, and especially not to have children with?" Yosika began crying over the phone and confessed that, "Yes, big brother, I do realize my big mistake now. I should not have acted the way I did. My big enemy has actually been, "ANGER!" Please forgive me," she mumbled. Yosika begged her big brother to act as her advocate. She asked him to beg her parents as well as everyone in the family, to have mercy on her. She said, "Please tell them to forgive me as God forgives every human being, unconditionally."

His brother promised that he will do it, "However, he told her, "you too on your side, you must pray sincerely to God; so that He can touch the heart of everyone in the family, who are actually heartbroken. You should also know that everyone is actually regretting to see you in such a predicament. Most of them are saying," Yosika switched her aspiration, from a prospective lawyer to nothingness! "This is awfully sad." Many individuals who had known her in the pass concluded as though they were perfect beings.

After having talked to her sister, the brother called his parents immediately, and chose to speak to his mother first. And then, he spoke to his father afterwards. He had begged them to forgive Yosika, and had prayed that God by his mercy to get his sister out of that confusion state..

The brother knew however, that his father had a hot temper, and therefore, he had to utilize biblical language in order to calm him down, because he was a strong believer in God. He told his father, "Dad, we are actually living in an imperfect world. Every human being is fallible, so is Yosika. Atondi, I understand has been evicted from his home. Further, I have been made aware that his relatives informed him that they are unable to assist him. Currently, Yosika and her two sons are staying at aunt Esperance's home. God bless her and her husband for having such degree of love. At the present time, I believe that God is testing our faith. Mom and Dad, I would suggest the following, if you will, to please allow Yosika and the children to stay by you just for a while; because there are two vacant rooms in the house. At first, Mr. Bala had showed some degree of reluctance, when he heard his son mentioned the idea of allowing Yosika and her children to move with them. However, because his son has prefaced his request using the word of God, that made a big difference in his mind. That sentence had actually touched his heart, and then, he accepted afterwards. He replied to his son, fine. We will let her and the children move in with us. However, Atondi will have to beg his relatives to accommodate him. Officially, the father said, "He cannot be considered as our son in-law yet, because he has not yet met any of his dowries' obligations. We must honor the norms of the Congolese society. Atondi cannot change our ancestors' principles," the father sounded stern.

Certainly, the son understood that every word his father had said was absolutely correct. However, he told the father, Dad, for the sake of his children, the French people say, "*Le vin est tiré, il faut le boire,*" (There is no going back now, we must face the music).

Considering the fact that Atondi is the father of Yosika's children, and based on the fact that he has just graduated from college, can you possibly accommodate all of them temporarily? Let's grant him six to nine months stay only until he finds a job and home to raise his children." Yosika's brother sounded very sympathetic, ultimately, he convinced his parents.

However, he insisted, Dad, please be stern. When Atondi comes in, please make him aware that while he is staying in your home, he should actually bear in mind that he has three obligations to meet: His first obligation would be to find an employment, and his second obligation would be to find a home, where he has to move in and raise his family. Then, his third obligation would be to honor our ancestors' principles; he must offer the dowries. Please,

Dad, he said,"Remind Atondi that he cannot escape his dowry's obligations in order to honor God, our family as well as our culture. In addition, when you speak to that fellow, try to sound severe in your language, so that he does not feel too comfortable in that big house, and overlook his manhood's obligations.

The parents accepted the advice of their son. And then, they had asked Yosika, the children and Atondi to come in and stay by them, on a temporary basis only. It was such a relief for Atondi, because after his eviction, he had absolutely no roof over his head. Atondi had absolutely no shelter that could accommodate him. Prior to moving in the in-laws' house, Yosika's parents advised their daughter that Atondi should be made aware of the following, "We are welcoming him to our house, however, he should remember the French people saying, "*Fais-toi comme chez toi, mais tout en sachant que tu n'es pas chez toi,*" this simply signifies that "*Feel at home nevertheless, do not forget that you are not really at your home.*" Yosika parents let them actually stay free of charge, because they were aware of their financial situation. As soon as they had moved in, they were advised that it was actually a temporary stay until you, the husband strives to find a job and a place to raise your children. Those were actually the terms under which Yosika's parents and Atondi agreed upon.

Atondi was so happy to stay in such a huge and spacious house. He actually brought some of his personal belongings in the room which they had been offered. The rest of his stuff was seized by the landlord because he did not meet his tenancy's obligations.

From the day that they had moved in Yosika's parents' home, every problem in terms of paying rent and buying food were actually dissipated from Atondi's head. Atondi had no more financial pressure. The in-laws took care of all their basic needs. They also adored their grandchildren because they were the very picture of their daughter, Yosika. Children were well fed and well dressed. One could actually tell the difference in terms of their development. However, Atondi was not exhibiting any effort to find any employment at all. That situation lasted for such a long time.

EPISODE 10

Atondi Turned Down a Job Offer Arranged by His in-Laws

Mr. and Mrs. Bala discussed the issue among them, and then decided to bring the issue to their best friend who worked for the Board of Education Department, in order to find Atondi a teaching job. Mr. Bala was known as a persuasive man. He told his friend that Atondi was a college graduate, and that he believed that he could actually teach junior high school or even elementary School, if need be; provided that he has some kind of occupation and income.

Mr. Bala went through all that trouble in order to arrange for Atondi to teach and keep busy until he finds a job in his field of study. Everyone in the family was excited that Atondi will be soon working, and that his boredom will be vanished in order to become productive. It was however appalling, to hear what Atondi had to actually answer regarding that job offer.

One evening, Mrs Bala's friend came by the house in order to meet with Atondi, and to arrange for a possible job interview. Everyone was excited to see that particular friend. When he came in that evening, every family member was present, including Atondi and Yosika.

And suddenly, Mr. Bala introduced Atondi to the said friend. They shook hands, and sat in the living room. Shortly afterwards, the friend asked Atondi," I understand that you studied Finance?" Atondi replied anxiously, "Yes, I did. However, I have not found any work in my field since I graduated." The friend asked Atondi, "How long ago was that?"

He answered that it has been seven years ago. The friend said to him, "Would you be interested in accepting a teaching position in the meantime until a position becomes available in your field of study?" Instead of rejoicing for that offer, Atondi's answered abruptly, "What, a teaching position?" He continued, shaking his head, "That actually would be an insult to my intelligence.

I would not belittle myself to such a degree by accepting such a low paying job. I studied Finance, and I must have a job in the field in which I received training. No thank you, sir, I just refuse your offer!" Atondi was furious, and he stood up, and walked away.

He was murmuring in his way, "A teaching job? How much would they actually pay me? The position pays close to nothing. That would be nothing, but wasting my precious time," he concluded. Every person who was present at that time, stayed spellbound as they watched him walking out. He actually went to take a stroll. What an embarrassment to the entire family, who expected a happy ending! The guest and the in-laws could not comprehend that weird reaction. They did not mean any harm but were just attempting to help him to start being productive, and contribute in nurturing his children. It seemed appalling indeed to all who had witnessed that incident.

Obviously, Atondi meant what he had said. He had never changed his mind for accepting that job offer. He had preferred rather to remain unemployed and continue to have free accommodations as well as being fed by his in-laws; just for the fact that they were well to do. Both, Mr. and Mrs. Bala were in their late fiftieth. However, they were known to be a hardworking couple. They had always left their house early in the morning and returned home around 4:30 p.m. Atondi on the other hand, rejoiced staying home all day long. He had developed a high degree of his leisure time. He felt at home and did whatever he wanted behind. And then, finally he would go out to take a stroll, around 4:20 p.m. or a few minutes prior to his in-laws' return from work.

He would then return home around diner time. Atondi had never had it so easy in his life time. He rejoiced exceedingly experiencing that kind of high class life, and he considered himself to be the luckiest man in the Congo. The expression, *African's man stamina* started to sound just another words to Atondi. It had no more impact in his mind, because all was provided for him and his family. Therefore he neglected to exert his own efforts to acquire his own as well as his family's basic needs. The fact that his in-laws adored his children was a big consolation and confidence for him.

Days went by so quickly, and yet, Atondi was not budging to find any kind of work. In fact, he had always come out with one special excuse, "Well I have been looking for work all this time, and nothing has been found in my field. Every time anyone would advise him to accept any kind of work that is available in the meantime. Atondi would actually take that advice as an insult; he would flare up with that individual. Atondi would address to any individual who would advise him to find a job or move out of his in-laws's house, very unkindly and without any reservation. He actually viewed that advice as being some sort of jealousy or offense.

Then, few years later, Yosika's brother called her from abroad again, in order to find out whether or not her husband's job issues had been resolved. Further, he also questioned her, "What is your time frame of moving out of our parents' house?" Yosika replied, "Well, Yaya or big brother", Atondi is still trying to find work, and, nothing has come up yet so far."

Apparently, Atondi showed no incentive in terms of finding work. He therefore had formed the habit of arguing with any outsider or even family members who would question him, "Are you still living with your in-laws up to this day?" Atondi actually hated this kind of remarks. He was always on the defensive side, because he was not ready to moving out. He hated the thought of worrying about paying the rent or buying food or clothing for children and wife. Those issues were out of his mind completely. So, he resented everyone who would touch that issue. Although, he was not a stammer, but, whenever that topic would be raised, Atondi would pretend to stammer in carrying out the discussion regarding this matter.

Ultimately, Yosika completed her training at the Beauty School. Finally, she began working part-time at the beauty school. In addition, she worked privately at some of her private clients' homes. Atondi on the other hand, had just stopped even doing his insignificant business activities which he used to conduct in the past. His former activities were, purchasing commodities in order to re-sell. This actually was no longer his incentive. Consequently, he became dependent completely upon, his father and mother's in-laws.

Atondi felt as though Yosika's parents were his own parents. It was an astonishing scenario, because living in the in-laws' home has never been a norm in the Congolese culture. It is rarely to see a man living in his in-laws. That was actually something which could only happen temporarily and on an emergency basis. Atondi however, broke the record, and overlooked the Congolese culture and its norms. This was so strange to everyone who hears about this situation. Everybody ponders to notice Atondi's absurd behavior.

EPISODE 11

THE IN-LAWS HOLD FIRST & SECOND MEETING WITH ATONDI.

Aleyi Atondi continued to live with his in-laws for a long time. And, then, five years later, the in-laws decided to have a talk with him for the first time. Yosika's father conducted that small meeting. He began by saying, "Aleyi, customarily a young man who decides to get married, must remember that, *he must be a bread winner for his family,* isn't that correct?" Instead of replying, yes or no, to the question asked, Atondi began crying, and then, all of a sudden, he shouted, *"Papa Bala, just give me the bottom line*. If you do not want me to continue being Yosika's husband, please, just let me know; instead of giving me a run around." At first, the children were in their bed room while the meeting had begun. However, as soon as they heard their father crying loud in the living room, they came out running towards the living room. Without asking the reason why their father was actually crying, they too, joined their father. They started also crying along with Atondi. It was observed that one son held his father's left hand, and the other held his right hand. Yosika on the other hand, had remained seated looking downward because the scene appeared to be appalling.

Noticing that chaos, Yosika's mother told her husband to interrupt the meeting that night, immediately. Therefore, the meeting was adjourned, Mr. Bala told everyone to return to their rooms. Atondi and the children let the living room, and then rushed to their room. Yosika stayed in the living room with his parents. Then, her parents faced her, and shook their heads, simultaneously. The mother said to her, "Yosika where did we go wrong?" We had a high expectation of you. You had a goal of becoming "Advocate" (lawyer), and that was actually the reason why we had allowed you to pursuit your education here, at the University of Kinshasa."

The father added, Yosika, if we had known that you were going to wind up with this kind of unnecessary relationship here in Kinshasa, we wouldn't have permitted you to come here. Now, how do you feel in finding yourselves in such a deplorable situation? Instead of being single and cope with your own life, you notice the burden you are now carrying? You have two children plus this man, and *his illegitimate son on* top of this scenario? The fact that you have been evicted now, what would you have done if we had not move to Kinshasa at this particular time? Have I ever done any such thing to your mother?" Her father questioned Yosika?

Yosika was unable to face her parents. Finally, she took the courage to say a word to her parents, saying, "I have to begin with an apology to you, Mom and Daddy. I understand your concern about this awful picture which you have been forced to watch. I am so ashamed of myself. Nevertheless, I do take the blame for allowing myself to get involved with this man. Actually, I do now realize that I should have communicated with you prior to this outcome; and ask for advice regarding the dilemma which stood between my school work and my relationship with both of my aunts."

Mrs. Bala interrupted her, and asked, "Where did you ever meet this gentleman, by the way?" She then, seized the opportunity to relate to them in details, the evolution of that particular relationship. "Her parents, especially her father became very upset to hear this entire story, and he said, "Yosika, you knew things were getting out of hands, and that would have been the time, you could have communicated with us. It is of course a big mistake that you had made of keeping this problem inside of you; and which was eating you up, like a "Mpuku" (Mice).

The father sounded authoritative as he talked to his daughter. However, he calmed himself down for a few minutes, and said to her, "By the grace of God, whom we believe in, we have no other alternative but to forgive you, daughter," he said to her. Then, her mother also added, because God is always forgiving everyone that trespasses, we also must do the same. However you must continue to encourage your so called husband and remember that, in our culture, a man is thought from his childhood, that *he must be a bread winne*r, and not be dependent upon his wife or his wife's family!" This is actually a fallacy! Mrs. Bala said, shaking her head left to right. No one has ever witness such a thing.

Nonetheless, we are glad that you took the stand of receiving an important training. That step shows actually that you are willing to take the responsibility of caring for your children. God is good indeed, her mother said. God actually wants every individual to exert his or her energy and ability in order to acquire what is needed in terms of making a living.

Yosika's mother continues we are however grateful to God for giving us healthy and beautiful grandchildren. Although, you had made a bad choice in terms of selecting a decent father for your children, nevertheless, the skill which you have just acquired, can make you successful in the future, if you so desire . You have the attributes which the public likes. Therefore, you can attract several good clients and have enough income to support your children in the future. Therefore, if this fellow continues to exhibit a laid-back attitude, thinking that shading tears consecutively in order to hide his indolence, would feed or clothe his children, and then, in that case, you would have to take a stand to make a decent and wise decision.

Remember whichever decision you make, it would have to be beneficial to you and to your children. As far as we are concerned, we sincerely believe that the best time of making that decision would be prior to marrying to him, the father concluded. If he thinks that the one bottle of palm wine he offered to your uncle Luzola sustains for marriage, he might as well forget it. How long he believes would take us to reimburse it?

Yosika was finally relieved from the burden of having concealed the motive which had led her to such false relationship with Atondi. Apparently, a relationship which was never meant to be as far as Yosika was concerned. She was grateful to God indeed for allowing her parents to forgive her. Ultimately, she admitted her big mistakes, and felt deep down inside that she was set free. Certainly, after that particular meeting with her parents, Yosika knew that her relationship with her parents had become genuine as it has been prior to getting involved with Atondi.

Atondi on the other hand, became conscious that his in-laws were becoming more concerned regarding his lethargy. Consequently, he started to spend more time outdoors and returned home around 6:00 P.M. instead of 4:30 P.M. as usual. Eventually, this was an alibi of making believe that he was out looking for work.

THE IN-LAWS HOLD A SECOND MEETING WITH ATONDI

Thus, two years after the last meeting, the in-laws decided to host another family meeting. Yosika was notified, then, she too informed Atondi. As usual, Atondi hated to hear the word "meeting." As soon as he was advised, as usual, Atondi became in a very bad mood. He put himself on a defensive side prior to the meeting. In fact, Atondi was the last person to appear in the living room that evening in order to attend the family meeting. It was observed that everyone had been seating for quite some time in the living room. He knew somehow that he was being confronted once more concerning his work situation.

However, the first question that his father's in-law had asked him was, "Aleyi, we are gathered here because we would like to know your short terms as well as your long terms goals with your family. Can you possibly tell us how do you plan to meet these goals?" Eventually, those questions were far from Aleyi's mind. He actually had no relevant answer. As a result, Atondi stood up spontaneously and replied, "*I do not comprehend this, why you should actually ask me such a question, when you know quite well that I do not have any employment*?" His father's in-la, evidently got annoyed to hear that tone of voice, so was Yosika's mother.

Shortly afterwards, the father in-law replied, "Apparently Aleyi, you are forgetting one thing. I should refresh your memory, in case you do not remember; "Every Congolese man is taught from his childhood that, a man is *a bread winner in his family*; if a man gets married, *he cannot live in his in-laws home*. He must provide a place for his wife and children, and this is how he actually exemplifies his maturity.

Aleyi don't you recall this cultural education?" His father in-law asked him. Further, he added, "I am quite sure your parents did mention this subject to you, as do the rest of Congolese parents." Furthermore, he continued, "Well, Aleyi after seven years that we have allowed you to reside here in our home, my wife and I feel that you actually must leave this house. Besides, you have brought with you, in our home, a son whom you have had with another woman. This boy is now 11 years old now. You actually had forced us to care for him as well. How do you actually expect your in-laws to continue providing for you and your illegitimate son? Shall we take care of Yosika as well as the two sons whom you are the father? Or shall we continue to take care of you, the father and your illegitimate son on top of it?" Please give us a simple answer, Mr. Bala questioned him.

Mrs. Bala added, Aleyi, we actually had thought that we would help you temporarily while you are attempting to find work, and subsequently, you would find a place to raise your family. If we had known that you would prove to be a sluggish man, we would have never accepted you in our home with your illegitimate son on top of all this chaos. It is actually inappropriate for a son in-law to continue living at his in-laws' home for such an extended time. We are therefore asking you at this point, to kindly depart from here.

By all mean, empower yourself. Seek to be self-sufficient rather than continuing to be a parasite. Please remember that this world is not a Paradise where all is provided you. I think it bears to remind you, the old saying, in Lingala language, "*Soki moto asali te, akoki kolia te*" (it means literally that "If a person does not work, he cannot eat as well)." The only way a man can get any food and a roof, would be in exchange with his labor. Otherwise, that shows that you are actually working against the laws of Nature. We cannot continue to tolerate this situation. It is inappropriate.

Mr.Bala continued, evidently, no one in this world can escape from God's Mighty words. He then referred Atondi to the book of "Genesis 3:19 - *In the sweat of your face shall you eat bread,*" – Mr. Bala told Atondi, this is actually a proof that our ancestors' expressions came from the wisdom of God. So do not think that my wife and I mean any harm to you. We are actually taking this action in order to help you to start taking initiatives in life; especially when you have produced children. You must recall that you can no longer be called *"YA BEBE"* (meaning, a Big Baby), but rather you are being called 'PAPA or Daddy."

Please believe us, Mr. Bala continued, that being called "Papa or Dad," this refers to a title of honor. It is a *HUGE TITLE* which comes with serious *Responsibilities* of caring for those whom God has put in your possession. Actually those are individuals who cannot help themselves, at the early stage of their lives. Therefore, if you neglect the above mentioned responsibilities, remember, from our Congolese Culture standpoint, you are regarded as a *FAILURE* or man who has actually lost his stamina. Furthermore, remember that we, Yosika's parents are not here to help you lose your *African's*

man Stamina, rather, we are here to empower you so that you can resume your Congolese man's STAMINA; and gain respect in the Congolese society," Mr. Bala concluded with an authoritative voice.

In a very calm voice, Mr. Bala continued, "As I had previously mentioned, our patience has come to its limit. We can no longer accommodate you here. However, you are being given one week to prepare your departure from here. Atondi did not expect that conclusion.

Suddenly, he busted crying loud, as usual. Since he was known to be very good with adulations, while crying, he added the following words, "Papa Bala, how can you ever tell me to move out? Where do you want me to go? I consider you, as my own parent; as you know my father and mother are now dead. How could you really decide to put me out?" Mr. Bala answered, "Aleyi you have been living here in this home for over seven years and half, and that is prior to the consecutive death of your parents in the village. Besides from this, you are now forty years old, and you cannot possibly continue to be living as a parasite. Furthermore, at the age of maturity, you cannot be dependent upon the in-laws or your wife. Everyone is criticizing our daughter, and we, her parents who are apparently fostering your peculiar demeanor. Eventually, you are not honoring the principles of our culture, so please do not even attempt to rationalize your conduct.

In fact, when the meeting was going on in the living room, the children were in their bed room. Shortly afterwards, they heard their daddy crying loud, as he had done previously. Then suddenly, both children come out again, rushing in the living room in order to verify what was going on.

As soon as Atondi noticed the presence of his children, again, he exaggerated his crying loud. Both children, simultaneously, joined their daddy. Shortly after that, together, they started crying in unison, each one of them held on of his father's hand. Every time that incident occurred, children were never actually made aware of the reason why their dad was doing so. As it had happened previously, the evening ended up in chaos. And therefore, the meeting was adjourned for the second time.

Thus, everyone was obligated to return to their rooms, except, Yosika and her parents. Three of them exchanged few words. The mother just gave Yosika a sad look, shaking her head, and saying "see daughter, the kind of life you now wound up with?" The mother whispered, Yosika, in life, you can never act or make any important decision when you are irritated." Her father added, "my daughter, I can confirm that anyone who has the propensity of making decisions while he or she is in a state of irritation, at the end, that individual regrets it enormously. Actually, it has been proven ninety nine percent that, that sort of reaction yields a wrong result or unpleasant consequences which cannot be remedied."

Yosika was facing the floor. Then she murmured, "Again I am really sorry for putting you in such unpleasant situation. I realize what you are saying to be absolutely true. Evidently, I now have learned my lesson. In the future, I will be cautious in terms of making any type of decision from now on, and never will I make any important decision, whenever I shall find myself in a fuming state of mind," she promised.

Mr. Bala, asked Yosika, "What Atondi has been doing really since you moved in this house? Yosika told her parents, Atondi has really disappointed me in terms of his indolence.

When I had met him, he used to do both, studying and doing some trading on a side. He knew how to take initiatives, and I do not quite comprehend why he had gotten too lazy? Her mother replied, "Well because he sees that everything is being provided him. He no longer has a rent to pay. In addition, he does not have to think about buying food or clothing for his children, and therefore, he feels very comfortable to remain here without having any family obligations to meet. Besides, he is not willing of making any move to improve his work status. In such a view, what future have you got, Yosika? Her mother asked. Then she continued, "Well, I believe that all we have to do is to continue praying, and let God guide us in resolving this seeming mystery."

Then Mr. Bala asked her daughter "Did Atondi make any more comments regarding the teaching position that he was being offered? Yosika replied, dad, Aleyi does not want to hear about it at all." Why not, her father asked?

She answered, "Well he feels that the pay is close to nothing. He also said that accepting that position would be a waste of his valuable time." Hearing this answer, her mother added, what did I just say? The man feels no pressure whatsoever, as a result, he prefers to utilize his time unwisely. Afterwards, Mr. Bala asked Yosika, how Atondi's daily schedule really is? Yosika replied, well, I do know that most of the time he goes either to his cousin, Belinda's place or sometimes, he goes to "Stade de Football" or (Soccer Stadium) in order to watch "the Soccer game." Is that a good vision for his wife and his children's future? Her mother asked Yosika, ironically.

0Evidently, Atondi continued to play his game with his in-laws for quite sometimes. He actually was convinced that the crying scam was working so well in order to disrupt the meeting with his in-laws. He was actually panic-stricken of taking the responsibilities of his own household expense. During all that time, Atondi's scenario spread out to almost all the neighbors, family's friends, and acquaintances. Eventually, everyone was concerned to notice Atondi's sluggishness and the fact that he continued to rationalize his excuses of not accepting any type of work that could help him in contributing in his in-laws's household expenses, or becoming self-sufficient.

EPISODE 12

Aunt Mutema Educates Children

Yosika's children adored aunt Mutema, so, every time she visited them at their grandparents' home where they were residing, the children will run towards her eagerly. She had the habit of bringing them little gifts. They loved those gifts exceedingly. She was also teaching them cultural education, and they were following it pretty well. Aunt Mutema had the ability to apply her pedagogy as well as methodology expertise to better teach the children gradually. Besides from teaching them Congolese culture, she also started to include the word of God. Aunt Mutema stressed more on three subject matters: God the Creator and (Jesus as well as the Angels), she also taught the children that the most dangerous things in life were: lying and stealing. Aunt Mutema teaching was based on this theme.

Aunt Mutema was so patient with her nephews. She was always explaining and answering their innocent and genuine children's questions. They would ask questions such as "What is lying mean? She would answer, "Lying is saying something that is not true. Esperance would also try to give them a tangible example, such as: "if I give you a piece of this orange," and she would actually give to each of them a piece of orange. Then, she would tell them to go ahead, and eat it, and they would actually eat it. Subsequently, aunt Mutema would tell them, now, I will explain to you the meaning of the world "Lying." She would ask them "Tell me what you have done with the piece of orange which I have just given you?" Both children would reply simultaneously, I ate it. And then, she would reply fine. You ate it right? Children would answer, "Yes". Supposing your grandmother asks you a question, "Did you eat any piece of orange today? What would you say to her? Each one replied, "I would say to her, "yes", I did eat it. Very good, aunt Mutema would reply. Then she would continue, "Now, if you had to answer to her that, "No", I did not eat it, that would be called "Lying." Her nephews would smile at her, and confirmed that they surely understood the meaning of the word lying.

One of the children would ask aunt Mutema, what happen if someone lies? Aunt Mutema would reply, "Oh! That is no good, because that person will be called a "Liar." God send all the liars to hell. A person, who tells the truth, will go to Heaven. Therefore, you must learn how to always tell the truth. Her nephews would be listening attentively.

Aunt Mutema would also stress on the word, "Stealing". She would explain to the children that the world "Stealing" means taking something that belongs to someone else, either by force or behind that individual's back.

To illustrate the fact, Aunt Mutema, gave to each child $1.00 (one dollar) bill, and she began to explain to them what the word stealing signified. She told them, "Now hold your money tight in your hand." She ordered the children to go and ask a container or an empty tiny box in order to hide their money. Their grandmother Bala gave to each boy a small empty can, in order to serve it as a piggybank. Suddenly, each of them brought his can to aunt Mutema. And then, she began to instruct them saying, "Now lift your money", carefully; they obeyed, following the instructions. Aunt Mutema explained to them, while you are holding you money, if somebody comes in, and takes your money from your hands, then run away with it, that means, "stealing." If you put your money in this can, and then someone comes in and breaks the money box, and then run away with your money, that means "Stealing." Stealing, she insisted, is actually taking something which does not belong to you.

Children would be listening alertly. Suddenly, one of them asked her, "What does he do with that money that person steals? She replied the individual who steals your money is called a "Thief". Usually, they are lazy people. They do not like to work, and they wind up stealing. And then, when they run away with your money, they can buy food or candies for their children. Esperance raised the consciousness of her nephews by informing them that the person who steals always take the consequences afterwards. She advised them, "Don't you ever accept or eat anything that was stolen from somebody else." Do you hear me? They children replied, yes.

One of the child asked "why not", she told the children, "It is because God does not want people to steal. That is the reason why, he gave us the brain to think. Further, he also gave us the hands to do any kind of work we choose to do, so that the individual can earn his money honestly. God is happy when we use the strength and the intelligence he gave us in a wisely manner in order to earn our living.

Esperance continued, our ancestors also had warned us not to eat or to accept anything that has been stolen, because it is extremely dangerous. It will cause a lot of problem in the future. God wants everybody to work, and earn their money honestly, and buy things that they need. Our ancestors also warn us not to pick up anything that you would find on the street. That thing or money belongs to somebody else. It is not yours, and therefore you should leave it alone. Don't you ever pick it up because you do not know its nature or its origin, O.K? The children nodded their heads.

Another child asked her, "Why should it be dangerous to accept or to eat anything that had been stolen from another person? Aunt Mutema explained it is very dangerous because it will bring you something calls, "*MALEDICTION*" *or a CURSE* that will last from one generation to the next generation. The children were seven and six years old at that time. They did not quite understand at the first time. They kept on asking every time they were with aunt Mutema, the educator, to talk more about stealing consequences.

Aunt Mutema would explain little at a time according to their level of understanding. She would start with plain examples, explaining gradually. Eventually, they began to grasp the meaning of the word, Malediction or Curse as they were growing. They started to receive extensive explanation regarding the misfortune which stealing or taking someone else belongings forcefully, could result in somebody's life. She would name things such as, failure in business, in marriage or even ill-health. That could easily last from one generation to the next generation.

Aunt Mutema also stressed on the fact that the children must learn the danger of having parents who confiscate other's people money or belonging in order to feed them, because this fact actually brings, what we call "Malediction" or Curse in the future. This education was well accepted by the children. The explanation of the topics of lying and stealing were embedded in those children's mind. In addition, the children would never pick up any money or item found on the street. That is a taboo for Congolese's culture, they would recall it. Children were actually taught that whoever who lost his or her money or item would eventually come back that way, and find it there.

Children also would take the opportunity to discuss the cultural education they have been receiving with their grandparents Bala. They too, would eagerly confirm the danger of stealing other people's finance or any other items whether in the house or outside.

Atondi was too much involved into himself. He did not devote any of his time to educate his own children. The boys had reached nine years old and could not relate anything that they have learnt from their father. Aunt Mutema was on top of their education. They were still being nurtured by their grandparents all that time.

EPISODE 13

Yosika Decides To Have a Talk With Atondi

Yosika on the other hand, was being questioned from left to right regarding her so called husband's irresponsibility. Based on that pressure, she too, would speak with Atondi privately in order to remind him that he ought to take initiatives, somehow.

She would remind him that, "Atondi, you are not getting any younger. Atondi, you cannot continue feeling comfortable to live with the in-laws for so long. Atondi would reply with an unpleasant tone of voice, "Yosika, do not underestimate me just because I am living at your parents' house. Didn't I offer you a shelter when you needed one?" Yosika would reply, "Of course, you did Atondi, but it was just for the duration of one year, then we were evicted, right after that. Again, Yosika would continue, "Atondi, we have been living at my parents' home for nine years now. It is actually time for us to move out of here. Children must follow after their father's foots steps. Everyone is worrying about your negative example. You have lost your Congolese man's resilience, and had replaced it by laziness. That is not a positive view to the children who are in the process of learning our ancestors' culture. She would also refer to her uncle Luzola's example. Yosika would tell Atondi, "You have been in my village.

Haven't you noticed the manner in which uncle Luzola worked? Didn't you notice how hard his assistants work? Haven't you noticed women and men selling the following items: basin of Fufu or Cassava, Mbika or Ntere (Pumpkin Seed), palm fruit, palm oil, dried fish, dried Mushroom and pepper to all those businessmen whose trucks were being repaired at my uncle' s shop, in the Farm? Atondi, if those men in the village could exert their energy to produce money in order to support their family, and I wonder why can't you?

Atondi would answer back to her unkindly, "It is not my false, and there is no job available." Yosika advised him, "I think it is preferably that you accept any kind of work for the time being, and keep busy so that you can begin contributing in some expenses. Atondi would be very upset with his wife for bringing out such discussion. His favorite answer has always been, "Yosika, "why are you making this situation such a big deal.

Your parents have money to provide for everything. It is not as though they did not have enough. Why are you really complaining about? Atondi would reply sarcastically. Atondi's unkind replies had always disturbed everyone, whether the family members or friends and acquaintances.

EPISODE 14

Yosika's Grandparents Visit Her Parents

Children Receive Education

Few months later, Mrs. Bala Parents came to visit them. Her father was a retired pastor. Mrs' Bala father was actually known to many as a man who feared God in every action he took.

The children were so eager to meet their great grandparents. Although they were in their eightieth, both of them were in their sound mind. Children felt comfortable to verify with their great grandparents, everything which aunt Mutema had taught them concerning "lying and stealing topics" as well as their consequences thereafter.

Their great grandfather would always take the bible, and would confirm the ancestor's wisdom regarding what they actually had to say about the topics of "lying and especially stealing." He would bring the similarity of Congolese ancestor's word and that of the word of God.

He and his wife would insist on the similarity of both words lying and stealing, and the consequences of STEALING or doing wrong to the owner of that item stole. The French people say, "Les Biens Mal-acquis ne profitent jamais," it simply means that the ill-gotten gains are never beneficial, sooner or later will bring serious problems in someone's life. So, the retired pastor taught his great grandchildren to make sure that they will not steal, or harm anyone, and snatch their belongings, once they grow up. Children, he would warn them, "Beware, of the "malediction or curse" which follows afterwards. That is actually, God's punishment.

Mrs. Bala's parents actually pitied their great grandchildren for having Atondi for a father, because he had never set any time aside to educate his own children. They were however, very grateful to their daughter Esperance for her devotion to that effect. Customarily, boys have to remember their father's advice when they grow up. Apparently, they will only remember great grandparents' education and that which they had received from aunt Mutema.

They were developing with honesty, respect and fear of "Malediction, or Curse, as well as having stamina to confront life in order to become self-sufficient.

Children were told, in life, a person must start life fresh. Nothing should be haunting you. It is necessary to utilize God's given stamina in order to succeed in life and not to be a sluggish man. Therefore, it is very important to go to school, and to concentrate in school matter, so that you can become well educated. In that way, you can attract well educated friends, and attract a very beautiful and educated wife.

You must follow our example, children. Whatever you desire in life, you must exert your God given energy and intelligence. Be cautious, and don't you ever find excuses of not being able to acquire what God had designed for you. Further, never be jealous or harm anyone, because if you do, God will punish you. The children were receiving a high degree of knowledge. Every evening they would gather around their great grandfather in order to ask more questions and learn from his wisdom.

Ultimately, children began to deplore their dad lack of constructive activity, as they have watched their grandparents Bala, leaving early every morning for work, and returning home around 4:30 p.m. They also started to recall all the instructions their great grandfather had been teaching them regarding, man's stamina. And therefore, they became aware that a man should have a daily constructive activity. He must acquire a good education. He ought to apply his knowledge and strength to be productive in the society.

The boys also remembered certain things which their great grandfather had been advising them, he said, "a man must exert his stamina in order to obtain money, because without money, a man cannot attract any woman to marry. Women dislike lazy and poor men because they are grouchy people, and they have nothing good to offer a woman. Therefore it is vitally important for a man to be self-sufficient. Those were the topics which the children had always discussed with their grandparents and especially the great grandparents at home.

Considering the fact children were attending school, and were listening to other kids talk about their fathers' occupation and also the fact that their fathers were always giving them some money prior to going to school so that they could buy cookies or candies during the break time. Atondi's children would stare at each other and would feel badly about their father who never worked since they were born. One day however, the younger child asked Atondi, dad how is it that you do not work? In our school, our friends' fathers work, but we do not know what to say to our teachers when they ask us what your father's occupation is? Atondi told the child, "Well, just tell them that the reason I do not work, it is because I could not find any work in the Finance field."

At that time, Yosika replied, Atondi you can always accept any kind of offer, until the position becomes available in the Finance Department. It is very embarrassing for the children, they actually have nothing positive to relate concerning their Dad. Atondi as usual did not appreciate that kind of remark from his wife. Atondi told Yosika, it is actually, you, your parents and your grandparents who are trying to bad mouth me to my children.

The younger child again, told him, "dad it is true, you can actually do any kind of work in the meantime even "POUSSE-POUSSE or a Carriage man. He continued, "So what dad, there is nothing wrong with that kind of job, provided that you earn your money honestly. Atondi was furious right after that incident, and he then decided to walk out. His son then followed him behind, dad, dad, he asked, are you now going to find yourself a "pousse-pousse" job? The father would not answer, and he kept on going. Apparently, it was an excuse to get away for the fact that he was being confronted by his children, and everyone else in the family.

Eventually, the children became aware that their dad was actually too proud to accept any employment outside of his field. One day, however, the children noticed an unusual scene. Their father actually came in with some money in his hands. Children got scared. They glanced at each other without saying a word. However, they were alert and had become conscious of the two awful words, "stealing and lying" based on the education they had recently received from aunt Mutema previously, and subsequently from their great grandfather, a retired pastor. Those two topics were well elaborated and stressed by both family members. Besides, the retired pastor also had had the opportunity to read from the book of II Thessalonians 2:7 to his great grandchildren every time he talked to them regarding the generation curses.

Eventually, none of the family member had made any comments regarding that money, but it seemed suspicious to all of them. However, the next day, early in the morning, when the children were about to leave for school, for the first time, Atondi called them, and handed a five dollars bill to each of them.

While the children were holding the bills, their father's voice spoke, and said to them, "here is the money. You can use it to buy candy in school or cookies or mikate during your school break.

Both children glimpsed at each other, they became frightened. All of a sudden, they dropped the bills, simultaneously at Atondi's feet. Finally, each one backed up immediately, holding their hands upwards with palms facing their father. The younger son had always been the outspoken boy. Suddenly, he screamed at his father, "Dad, where did you get that money from? You do not work but, but...where this money came fro...m? Right after that, the older son added, "Oh, Dad we have been taught that when you see money in the hands of a person who does not work, we cannot hold or use that money. I am sorry Dad, we just cannot take it. Please Dad, if you found it on the street, please take it back if the same spot you found it. If it was looted, please bring it back to its owner. Atondi knew the truth behind his sons' words; however, he questioned them, "Why can't you take the money?" Both children replied, because the money that is not earned honestly is called "*BLOODY MONEY*". Dad, the Bloody money is extremely dangerous. It brings "Malediction or Curse in life. Also, we were told that "that curse" will always last from one generation to the next generation.

Suddenly, the younger son, screamed, "The curse" will actually bring unsuccessful business, and further, that person will remain poor during his entire life, because the bloody money or ill-gotten gains would ultimately flies away in the long run.

Then, the older son added, yes, Dad, the curse also brings ill health; and places barriers in people's way. Atondi was so amazed to hear his children reciting these well known facts. He then asked them with an authoritative voice, "Who ever had told you all these things?" Both children replied in unison, aunt Mutema, grandparents Balas and our great grandparents. They also confirmed that that advice came from our ancestors.

Further, great grandfather told us also that God told our ancestors to pass this knowledge to their children who will continue to pass it on to the future generation. Great grandfather had explained to us also that our ancestors insisted that every family member must warn their constituents not to feed children with stolen money or anything that came from any wrong source, because that brings a *"Malediction" or a CURSE* in the long run! Again, all of a sudden the children said in unison, with their eyes wide open, *"DAD, PLEASE STOP FEEDING US THE BLOODY MONEY BECAUSE THE BLOODY MONEY* BRINGS GENERATION CURSES!" Suddenly, both children took their school bags, and rushed out, one after the other, leaving their father behind. He stood there speechless, and watched them go. As soon as Yosika perceived the boys walking alone, she rushed out of the living room, and joined them. Atondi stood immovable, staring at the children as they proceeded. Finally, he collected the money that the children threw on the floor.

In fact, as soon as their mother open the door, the younger son, the bold one, turned towards his father and shouted, " Eh! Dad, remember when you die, please take that bloody money with you to hell. Please do not leave it for us, because we do not want to go to hell. We must begin our lives fresh, and spotless.

We do not want anything pursuing us. Everybody had warned us that this kind of money is very dangerous; if you do not earn it from your own labor. Aunt Mutema knows it. Grandparents Bala agreed with her, our great grandparents also confirmed it repeatedly.

Furthermore, our teachers in school told us the same thing. Atondi was left spellbound. He could not possibly imagine that his children had already been thought the cultural education which is normally thought by a father. He wondered how Yosika's parents and grandparents viewed him as a father who cannot educate his own children, or set any positive example. In addition, Atondi had realized that eventually, in the future, his children will be referring more to the education they have received from their mother's side than from their father's. He had no idea how he could possibly remedy those facts. Eventually, he felt guilty for proving to be an unreliable father.

The great grandparents were so proud of themselves for having transmitted God and the ancestors' knowledge to their great grandchildren. They also felt that they had actually been honored to hear the children defending themselves against the dishonesty and lying activities which are known as the most crucial topics in a Congolese's cultural education.

The great grandparents decided that while they were still visiting, they would continue to educate the children, not only Yosika's children, but all the children living in that house including Atondi's illegitimate son. The great grandfather was so gifted indeed in terms of teaching children. And his pastoral attributes were still embedded in him. He enjoyed empowering children, and preaching the word of God to them. He would repeat the topics of

Stealing, Lying, and he also would add other subjects such as "Anger and Peace, Justice and injustice, Respect and disrespect. He would also contrast Lethargy opposed to Stamina. He would teach the children to be strong and not lazy in life. He would illustrate two perceptions of a Congolese man in our society; the one who actually exhibits a stamina behavior and the man who exemplifies lethargic behavior. Great grandfather would whisper, "Children let me tell you a secret, remember that lethargy and stigma or dishonor are not God's qualities, but stamina or strength and determination, plus honor are what we call God's attributes. Those are the qualities you will be seeking in life if you want to be happy in your life, you understand? All the children will start nodding with a smile in their faces.

Mr. and Mrs. Bala were so glad that their children's great grandparents came to visit them. They were rendering a tremendous help in terms of children's education. They had actually enhanced aunt Esperance's ability. In addition, children had also learned how to read the word of God from the Bible. He also taught the children how to say their prayers at different occasions.

EPISODE 15

Great Grandparents Preached To Great

Grandchildren and Family

Considering the fact that Atondi was a hot-tempered man, the Pastor and his wife were concerned about the generational curse which their great grandchildren might inherit from their father.

Therefore, they could not help focusing their teaching on what the Bible teaches regarding "Anger". Due to this reason, every Saturday evening, the ex-pastor and his wife had formed the habit of preaching to all the children in that house. The children represented some sort of a tiny congregation to their great grandparents who spent all their lives ministries. The great grandfather actually would be eager to read from the following books and verses.

> *Proverbs 19:11, "A man's wisdom gives him patience; it is to his glory to overlook an offense."*

> *Proverbs 20:3, "It is to a man's honor to avoid strife, but every fool is quick to quarrel*

Proverbs 21:19, "Better to live in a desert than with a quarrelsome and ill-tempered wife."

Proverbs 22:24-25, "Do not make friends with a hot-tempered man, do not associate with one easily angered, or you may learn his ways and get yourself ensnared."

Proverbs 29:22, "An angry man stirs up dissension, and a hot-tempered one commits many sins."

The great grandfather would break down every word and simplified it in order to make the children understand the reason why they should not be hot-tempered or associate with such people. He would insist on the fact that, it is God's will. Further, he would focus on maintaining a happy attitude because that produces Peace and God is actually PEACE he would conclude.

As a result, those children became enlightened by their great grandparents' edification. It was amazing how the younger boy, who was known to be bold and outspoken, began to behave.

And therefore, whenever he was tempted to blow out like his father Atondi, the rest of the children would remind him, "Remember what great grandparents had just taught us on the subject of anger?" So, the boy would just touch his chest, and confirm 'Oh, yes I do recall now; anger is not God attribute. I do not want to be hot tempered like my father. No wonder, nobody wants to offer him a job. Isn't that a curse?" We shall verify it with great grandfather, the rest of the children would conclude.

EPISODE 16

Atondi Fails to Explore Business Opportunity

As years went by, Yosika began to feel very awkward for the fact that Atondi could not take any initiatives to find any sort of occupation. Finally, great grandparents requested a family meeting with Yosika's parents and herself. The decision was to try Atondi out, to give him some money so that he could begin traveling from the city capital to his village in order to conduct some trading activities. Atondi was called and instructed to begin some trading activities. The money was given to him. One part of the money was for his round-trip ticket and his personal needs. Another part of the money was for trading activities. Atondi was eager to accept the money. He then promised to depart and to return back to Kinshasa within two weeks time.

While everybody had believed that Atondi had travelled out of town, and that he was expected to return within two weeks, amazingly, Atondi was back after one week.

He came back without any single item in his hand. The children were eager to see him back. However when they had attempted to give him a hug, Atondi pouched them aside. Apparently, he was in a bad mood. When Yosika returned from her part-time job from the beauty salon, she perceived Atondi in the house. She wondered how is it that he returned earlier than it was expected. Nevertheless, she had made an attempt to approach him as well. However, Atondi spoke explicitly to her, "listen make sure that you do not start bombarding me with unnecessary questions, such as why and how, and so on." Children stared at their mother, and suddenly they shrugged. One of them started to rub his hands, and another had his hands crossed above his head. Yosika refrained from questioning him at that particular moment. After diner, however, everyone was eager to find out how things went? Atondi stoop up and replied, "Well, actually it was not possible for me to travel, so I delegated a cousin whom I trust so much; since he was returning to the village, I just gave him the money to purchase some commodities. I am therefore waiting for his return, with the stuff. Everyone was shocked to hear such an invalid excuse. There were no comments on the part of the in-laws. Everyone just glanced at each other as Atondi walked away.

However, privately, Yosika could not help following up into that situation. She told him "Aleyi, you have been gone for one week. Haven't you? You were given a round trip ticket as well as the money for your personal expenses. Is there any apparent reason why you chose to give that money to your cousin instead of going, and do business in person?" Atondi eventually hated this kind of confrontation.

He flared up, and responded with unpleasant language, such as, "I do not appreciate you implying that I actually have stolen your parents' money.. Do not be puffed up just because I am staying at your parents' home. I too, did give you a shelter when you needed one. Yosika answered to him, "Aleyi, at your apartment, we were evicted after one year of our relationship." She continued, prior to giving birth to my younger son, I and my first son used to spend most of our time at my aunt Mutema's home. She took care of me, my first son as well as my pregnancy care. Aleyi, she continued, do not forget that so far you have been living at my parents' home for over seven years now. You have been indolent for all this time. My parents have been willing to restore your activities by giving you money to begin some trading business. By the love of God, Aleyi your demeanor would have been courteous. You should have proven your African man's stamina as our culture requires it. Aleyi, why have you decided to embarrass me before my parents and my great grandparents? How would you ever have money to honor the dowry ceremonies that you owe to my family?"

Moreover, she said, "Do not forget that in the eyes of God as well as those of my family, you and I are not known as a married couple. Obviously, you are actually taking advantage of my family, because you are being allowed to reside in this house, where you are receiving better and free accommodations. You should however remember that, you are here just for the sake of the children. Therefore, you cool your temper, and begin creating harmony. Further, you also know that based on the Congolese cultural education, there would be no Congolese woman who could actually put up with a lethargic man.

In addition, no woman in the world would like to associate with a hot-tempered man either. I understand that no one is infallible in this world. And therefore, if there seems to be any issues, it would be preferably to resolve them wisely by establishing a clear communication. And a good communication represents a weapon that can dissolve any confusion among individuals without creating unnecessary tension with your close associations."

Yosika continued, "My great grandfather had been teaching children. And that include every one of us in this house to avoid ANGER and begin establishing PEACE, because anger is actually a sign of weakness, and it results to nothing positive, except tension. And what good can it do to a family?" Atondi kept quiet while Yosika took the authority to talk to him at that moment.

Yosika Bala continued, "Obviously, there could be no future between a wife and a husband, so called, when anger stands between them. In addition, she said, "A good father must be gentle to his children, and must also learn how to create a harmonious relationship with them. Aleyi, you have a shelter today because of these children. How could you possibly chase the children away when they had made an attempt to greet you joyously?" Yosika continued "Remember that you owe an apology to my children, because you have created a discordant feeling inside of them." Atondi, then, replied, well, I think it is good for them, because the children are getting arrogant with me. They have been talking about the bloody money. They talked about my temper and so on. Whoever has been telling them all these negative stuffs" he asked?

Yosika replied, "Well, the children are receiving cultural and religious education at the same time. Normally, it is the father's duty to educate his children. When would you ever teach these children things which they will remember one day when they grow up? What good examples are you actually setting for your children? By just sleeping, waking up, eating and taking a stroll daily, could things of that sort be a good education to the children? My parents and my great grandparents are obviously concerned about the future of their great, or grandchildren.

In fact, the so called Atondi's cousin to whom the money had been given in order to purchase the commodities in the villages, was never returned back to bring those goods as Atondi had promised. Atondi had never wanted anyone in the family to ever inquire about that money or about his cousin whereabouts. Therefore, after noticing the tension that was increasing around the family, the great grandfather began gathering every family member, almost every evening. He had begun preaching to the family about forgiveness. He actually started reading verses from the Holy Bible on "Forgiveness" as God teaches us. He used to focus his reading in the book of: Matthew 6-14-15, "For if you forgive men when they sin against you, your heavenly Father will forgive your sins."

Both great grandparents taught the children "how important it is to forgive others as we have been forgiven by the blood of Christ."

The word of God was proven to have a divine power that could transcend all that tension that was attempting to dominate the atmosphere of that house. However Mrs. Bala told her parents that "My husband and I, upon listening to the word of God, we have decided not to ask the money back from Atondi, just for the sake of the children. It is obvious, that he had spent it all. As usual, he refuses to engage himself in a different field, except finance, which he studied.

We would, however like to ask him to move out of our house, and find a place for him and his illegitimate son. Besides, we do not wish Yosika to have another child with such a lethargic man. They agreed with the idea of compelling Atondi to move out without any resentment.

Yosika's parents had promised to use their wisdom and good judgment in whichever approach they would take to dismiss Atondi. In regard to forgiveness, the retired pastor clarified that forgiveness does no actually entail or even replace a man's willingness to be productive. We cannot therefore, continue to encourage his negatives attributes, by all means. This fellow has been attempting to take advantage of our love for his children. Loving his children should not be regarded weakness." He should be proven wrong, they insisted.

One evening however, after the parents called Yosika in order to advise her about their decision to put Atondi, he was again called for the third time at the family's gathering. Mr. Bala began speaking, then Mrs. Bala concluded, saying, "Atondi after all this time we have given you to get yourself together, you have unfortunately failed our efforts. We therefore can no longer keep you here. We have forgiven everything you have done around the house.

We are now asking you to move from our home, and that is without any hard feeling." Upon hearing that crucial decision, as usual, Atondi busted crying, and pleading, "Papa and Mama Bala, you have replaced my parents who are now dead. You know very well that I have no other home, please revise your decision."

Mr. Bala asked Atondi, "How old are you now? Aren't you forty years old now? How much longer you want us to babysit you here?" Atondi replied, I promise Papa Bala and Mama Bala, let me remain here, I will soon find a job in the Finance Field, and I will help you out with the household expenses. At that time, Yosika children were sleeping deeply, but Atondi's illegitimate son was already fifteen years old at that time. And he came out of the room, and stood next to his father, tears dreaming down. He stood there without saying a word.

The in-laws ordered him to return to his room. That situation has become such a dilemma to the entire family; and even Bala's neighbors became frustrated the fact that Atondi had continued to live at his in-laws' expenses, for years without taking any kind of initiatives of becoming self-sufficient.

EPISODE 17

Yosika Decide to Move To South Africa

The whole situation became unbearable for Yosika. Finally, she had a talk with her parents. She told them that she wanted to move to South Africa and see if she could find a job

there. Yosika was known from her childhood as a very motivated girl. She was growing up with the same stamina. Her parents trusted that she will do well even in South Africa. Therefore, she gathered all the money she had earned from her part-time job as well as the tips she was receiving from her private clients. Thus, she told Aleyi, one day, that I must leave Kinshasa because life cannot continue in this manner. My parents had taken the burden of me, my two children and you as well as your illegitimate son for nine years. Evidently, no other parents can tolerate such thing. It has been very embarrassing for me. It is against our Congolese culture, as you know it well.

Further, it is against God's will. I feel so badly for my parents and especially for my great grandparents at their old age. They would have wanted to see Yosika's marriage ceremonies; traditional as well as religious which would have made them so proud of their granddaughter. But, Aleyi, examine the life that you had actually offered me! Everyone has been scoffing at me and at my family. I therefore, made a decision to go to South Africa immediately. Aleyi got nervous. He could hardly swallow that piece of information. He was panicky. Finally he asked her, "Are we going together with the kids?" No she replied. I just have enough money for my ticket, and some money for my stay. I am going to observe the situation. I am actually going to seek for work. If I do find a job, I will save enough money to send you so that you too, can join me afterwards with my two children. Concerning your illegitimate son, he will have to stay with his own mother," she concluded.

So Yosika was determined, and then left Kinshasa for South Africa. Upon arriving, she stayed by a friend, who helped her to get a working permit. It was not easy as in any foreign country. She spent all her money attempting to finance in getting her legal papers. Yosika was so organized that she found a job through a friend at the beauty salon. Yosika's talents and attributes spoke loud. Clients adored her style, and she started to make decent money. She kept her promise, and therefore, she saved $5,000 dollars in a short time. So, she contacted her parents, and informed them that she was sending $5,000 (five thousand dollars) for both children and Atondi to make travel arrangements, and join her within two months. In addition, she made sure to advise her parents to help Atondi with travel arrangements until its completion.

EPISODE 18

Atondi Failed To Make Travel Arrangements.

Atondi, however, upon receiving that money, he kept it a secret. He spent the money unwisely. He had thought it was so easy to just gather such an amount of money in Johannesburg in such a short time. For Atondi, that had actually been the first time to hold such a huge amount of money in his life. Therefore, instead of focusing on making travel arrangements as it was agreed upon with Yosika, he went wild in his imagination. Atondi used the money for entertaining his female friends. He was seen in different boroughs, eventually with different women. The in-laws could hardly see him around the house, since he received the money.

It was reported that that he had formed the habit of buying fresh fish from the sea ports in order to bring to his mistresses, because fish was his favorite dish. He continued to have banquets with his female friends. Consequently, the money was exhausted. Out of the $5,000 that Yosika had transferred, Atondi had only purchased one passport. It was just for him alone. He was unable to buy passports for his two boys. Therefore he had to stop making travel arrangement altogether.

Yosika had been under the impression that everything regarding travel arrangement was in readiness, because as far as she was concerned, she had sent enough money to cover all the necessary expenses. Unfortunately, she found out that besides from the one passport which cost him $100.00 (one hundred dollars) out of $5,000, Atondi did absolutely nothing else in terms of preparing the children's trip. On the contrary, Atondi started asking Yosika to send additional money in order to resume the travel expenses. After contacting her parents to inquire about the evolution of the travel arrangements, they were quite surprised to find out that the money had already been sent to Atondi, and yet, he had kept it a secret.

When the in-laws confronted him, he flared up as usual because he knew he had no legitimate excuses. And therefore, in order to save himself from embarrassment, he began returning home very late. His favorite time was after zero hour.

At that time, he was convinced that everyone was already in bed. He also made sure to get up early, in order to be the first one to live the house, around 6:00 a.m. so that he would not face any family member, who might inquire about this matter.

The children could hardly see their father around the house, since the departure of their mother to Johannesburg. It was a heartbreaking experience to the children, because their mother had promised them that they actually will meet in a short while. Further, she had assured the children that she was going prior to their arrival in order to prepare a place to receive them when they will join her. The children noticed however that it was taking longer than they had expected. And, therefore, both little boys started to become very anxious. In addition, they began bombarding their grandparents with questions concerning the date of their departure to South Africa. The children's favorite question to their grandparents used to be, "When are we supposed to depart to South Africa in order to join mama? Their grandparents would answer that you should actually address that question to your father, Atondi. The children would tell their grandparents that "We do not get to see our daddy, where did he go?" They would appear puzzled, looking at each other. Eventually the grandparents were disturbed to see children in this confused state. And therefore, they decided to call Yosika, and advised her to communicate with Atondi clearly because the children are inquiring about this matter. They ought to know the truth at this point. He must tell them explicitly whether or not they will actually travel? Furthermore, he must specify the date of travel in order to calm them down. Children are so anxious to travel. They had already spread the news to their classmates'.

Again Yosika called Atondi to inquire about this subject. Atondi, resented any confrontation of any kind, and therefore he got annoyed. Subsequently, he replied sarcastically, "Yosika, just send another $5,000 (five thousand dollars) so that I can proceed with travel arrangements. You might as well forget about the first amount you have sent. It was not enough to make any travel arrangements. That money is already gone! Do you hear me? I say, the fund has been crashed! That is the bottom line, Atondi said. Then, he hung up the phone. Yosika became very frustrated because she had worked extremely hard in order to save that amount of money. She had actual deprived herself from acquiring some of her personal needs, because she was really determined to come out with that amount of money. It was primarily for the sake of her children. In addition, it was to alleviate the burden of rearing her sons from her parents. Furthermore, it was to free her parents from sheltering and feeding Atondi's and his illegitimate son as well.

Yosika could not possibly comprehend the reason why Atondi, could not have seized that opportunity to leave the in-laws' house, once for all, and gain some degree of dignity? Yosika could not help weeping to find herself in such a predicament. It was hard to believe that Atondi would spend the full $5,000 unwisely! Yosika complained to his parents, "Atondi actually thinks that it is just so easy to acquire such amount of money in a short time here, in Johannesburg? She continued, Mom and Dad believe me if I were able to come out with that amount of money in a short time, it had actually been, because of the following reasons: The Beauty Salon had wealthy clients.

I was working very longue hours, and the clients were very pleased with my service. Therefore, they tipped me accordingly. Currently, the Beauty Salon where I used to work, underwent a change. It is now being run under a new Management. I am now needed only as a part-time employee. And therefore, it would not be possible for me to send Atondi an additional $5,000 which he is requesting.

Her parents were annoyed eventually, and advised her to call Atondi for the second time, and asked him to give you valid reasons regarding the previous five thousand dollars. She called Atondi again, in order to double check with him, what had he done with the previous $5,000? Atondi again found all sort of unkind words to address to Yosika. As usual he failed to give her legitimate reasons.

Ultimately, in order to create confusion between Yosika, her parents and aunt Bala, who is her father's sister, Atondi would run to aunt Lesa Bala, and he would invent all kind of false excuses to complain about Yosika's behavior. He told Lesa Bala that, "Yosika had been speaking to me with no respect since she had been in Johannesburg; probably she plans to marry another man." Please, do your best to stop her from taking that approach, because we have two children to rear as you know. Atondi, however did not mention anything to Lesa Bala regarding his abuses, nor did he imply that he actually had ruined the plan of travelling along with the children to South Africa.

Yosika's parents felt badly, the fact that their daughters' plans to join with her children were disrupted. The in-laws apparently, disapproved Atondi' mannerism and therefore, renounced to lay out any money for Atondi to join Yosika in Johannesburg, because he proved to be irresponsible husband and father. This actually was a strategy to prevent their daughter from having a third child with Atondi. As a result, they chose to continue rearing their grandchildren. The boys continued to attend school. They were well fed and well dressed. Atondi on the other hand, was puzzled. He could not believe seeing that awkward picture. He continued to call Yosika to act immediately in forwarding the fund. However, Yosika had hardened her heart because of that man's dirty game. She continued to remind him that, "Atondi, I have done my part. The ball is now on your camp. If you still want to join me along with the children, then use the previous five thousand dollars which I had transferred. If you have however spent it unwisely, well then, in that case you have no more reason of continuing to leave at my parents' home.

Atondi found reason to continuing living with the in-laws. He claimed however he was taking care of the children. He made Yosika believed that he walks the children to and from school daily. Further, he confirmed that the in-laws have no time to take care of that matter. Furthermore, he told her that the in-laws even give him the money to go and pay for the kids' tuitions as well as buying them school supplies. The fellow was quite slick, and he found a reason to ask Yosika for money, under the guise of alleviating from the in-laws the burden of paying for children's tuitions and other needs.

Yosika was fooled so many times by Atondi's mischief. She was not wise enough to notify his parents about the money she was sending to Atondi in order to help out with her children's needs. The money that Atondi was receiving from Yosika, he used it for his personal needs, without mentioning it to his in-laws. The children's needs were always provided by the in-laws.

Because he was so obsessed with the desire to impress his mistresses, Atondi made a serious mistake. The money he was receiving from the in-laws in order to pay for the children's tuitions, and purchase their school supplies, he started to use it for his personal needs, and eventually for entertaining his mistresses. So, every time the kids would go to school for the first day of class, the boys were being sent back home, because the tuitions were never paid. And therefore, they were not allowed to attend class.

Both kids used to return home with a note from the Principal. Once, Atondi and the kids' grandparents were absent at that time except the great grandparents, when the children came back from school weeping, saying, "We were chased from school. We could not get in the class, because, you did not pay our tuitions. They handed each a note that was given to them by the principal. The great grandfather read the letter, and kept them away in order to show to their daughter, Mrs. Bala and her husband, the children's grandparents. 7

As soon as Mrs Bala and her husband had arrived, they were notified. Everyone was depressed to notice Atondi's naughtiness. They exclaimed, we are actually tired with this fellow's monkey business. Therefore, the whole family decided to wait for his return, so he could be confronted. After zero hour, he arrived. So, they called him half an hour later after having his late diner in order to inquire about the tuition's issues. Atondi was a man who never admitted his false. He flared up as usual, answering "I did not steal the money. I just did not have the time to go pay the tuition, and besides the money is not enough to pay for the tuition," he said. Mrs. Bala then asked him, "Can you bring that money to us so that we can take care of this matter ourselves? Atondi, left them seating in the living room, and went to his room. They heard him crying because he knew that the money had already been spent, and that he had nothing left to present to his in-laws and their parents.

Mrs. Bala turned to her father, a retired pastor, and complained, saying, "Dad you have been preaching to us about God's patience and forgiveness. How can anybody tolerate Atondi's misbehavior? The retired pastor replied, "Child that is one of the challenges that a man has to face when living in this world. Retired pastor told his daughter, Mrs.Bala to call Yosika in Johannesburg, and tell her that, you who had brought this fellow here, in this house, here is what he has done. He continued, "My daughter, make sure to relay this issue to her. Further ask Yosika to inform us her ultimate decision regarding this issue."

Yosika disclosed to her family the details regarding the money she had been sending concerning the children's needs. She admitted sending money to Atondi in order to take care of the kids' tuitions and other needs. 1

She also told them that the primary reason for that action was to lessen the kids' expenses or burden from the family. However, she regretted taking such an action without notifying her folks. She said, "If I had known that Atondi is still acting as a "YA BEBE" or a Big Baby, who just refuses to grow up, and face the reality of his life, I would have sent that money directly to you, Mama and Papa." She continued, saying, " I must admit again, I have made another awful mistake. Please forgive me, I have learned from another hard lesson; and never will I get fooled by Atondi again in this matter. Further, I am actually surprised to hear that Atondi was still receiving money from you under the guise of covering the same children's expenses. Since he continues to dishonor you, I would suggest that you chase him and his son out of that house. Let him go out and learn that the world is not a paradise, where everything should be falling on his lap without any endeavor.

Yosika said, "Grandfather, please pray for me so that God will have mercy on me, and forgive me for allowing you to put Atondi and his illegitimate son out. I think God will understand the situation we have been going through. Her grandfather replied, "Yes, mama Yosika, (yes darling Yosika), this world, you see, it is a small planet in the eye of God, because He is the one who created it. He knows how everything and everyone operates in it. However, from a human being's perspective, it is actually huge, and therefore you cannot assume how an individual would act, the next minute. They say that "the human mind is just like a Monkey, because it jumps from one branch in one second, and it will jump to another branch in the next second.

Therefore, he continued, "If you desire to grow up until you will reach my age, my genuine advice would be to talk with God. And as a matter of fact, whatever you do, whether you are sleeping or waking up, and even you are eating, you should do it all with God, my grandchild. Please remember that always. In fact, your parents can talk to you million of times. I, your grandfather may advise you thousands of times, but the decision would have to be yours. You actually may pretend to hear what we have said to you. Nevertheless, you may ultimately choose not to implement anything you have heard from your family members. However, when God, who created every cell of your body, begins to speak to you, child, your stubbornness would have to be dissolved, no matter what it is." He continued, Yosika, this would be my genuine advice, which I will leave with you; whenever the Lord calls me back home, after my earthly pilgrimage." Yosika was completely touched to hear such a profound advice, from her grandfather. She also concluded that she was privilege to have a grandfather that was well inspired, and who exhibited full of wisdom.

ATONDI REAPS THE CONSEQUENCES OF HIS BEHAVIOR

Atondi on the other hand, since his latest confrontation with his in-laws, he began to return home around 12:45 A.M. a little later than he did previously. He was actually terrified by the idea of being put out of the in-laws' house completely, along with his illegitimate son. He did not know where to begin?

However, the in-laws felt that, as long as he has not moved out yet, out of their compassion, they felt obligated to continue feeding him by God's mercy. Therefore, food was being left for him to eat whenever he returned home. Since he has been living in that house for such a long time, Atondi carried himself as though he was a genuine family member who deserved any family share. Whenever he came back home, he would go in the kitchen directly, and help himself prior to going to bed. Concerning his illegitimate son, he was always fed and taken care of in a usual manner with the rest of the children.

Yosika grandparents decided to return back to their village after six months stay. They advised their daughter, Mrs. Bala and her husband that whatever decision they will make on Atondi's behalf, whether to put him out of the house, or any other, they reminded them to ensure the children safety, therefore proceed harmoniously. And the couple respected the senior citizen's advice. They realized that they were indeed full of wisdom.

Up to these days, Yosika's parents are still remembering the retired pastor's advice. They have been using God's wisdom; which is to remain calm, and continue to be patient with Atondi, until the children are big enough to be permitted to travel alone, and join their mother without being accompanied by Atondi. Currently, children are attending school as usual. Aunt Esperance Mutema continued to come by the house in order to tutor them. Yosika had formed the habit of calling them on a regular basis in order to follow up with their school progress.

The appalling thing is the fact that up to these days, Atondi at the age of forty one years old is still living at his in-laws' house. He remains without any ambition while all his friends had worked so hard to expand their perspective. Yosika, on the on the other hand, concluded that the relationship with Atondi was never meant to be. So, she decided to have nothing to do with Atondi anymore. As far as she is concerned, her relationship with Aleyi Atondi has ended. Aleyi Atondi has actually missed his opportunity once for all. Atondi made a history in the life of an African man. He is the well known Congolese man who had lost his male's stamina.

Conclusion

As we have noticed the episodes in the life of Atondi and Yosika. It is appalling to read that Mr. Aleyi Atondi, although he is viewed to be a healthy and strong man, unfortunately, because of his pride and anger, he continued to reside with his in-laws, while Yosika has taken residence in other country.

As an African woman, she has exemplified her ancestors' wisdom. She had acquired all the necessary tools to cope with social dilemma. She had been made aware that an African man must exert his resilience in order to support his wife and children appropriately. Besides, the man has no right to claim that he is married to that woman, if he had failed to honor his dowry's obligations.

And therefore, in life, it would be preferable for everyone to learn how to communicate with their associates in clear and precise manners, in order to prevent bad consequences. Further, the circumstances in which an individual finds himself or herself are served as testing areas sometimes which could help a person to grow from it.

And therefore, it is up to the individual to use his or her own judgment in making appropriate selections, which could result to a future misfortune. In addition, it would be necessary for people to remember that pride and anger should be regarded as the greatest enemies of every individual in this world, because both might lead us to reap nothing but failure in life.

FINIS

Africa Presents

- The Congo RDC and Lingala Language (English and French version (First edition) - **LINGALA/ENGLISH/FRENCH DICTIONARIES**

- The Congo RDC and Kikongo Language (English and French version (first edition). **KIKONGO YA L'ETAT/ENGLSIH DICTIONARY**

- The Congo RDC and Child Education (First edition)

- The Congo RDC and Congolese Cuisine (First edition)

- The Congo RDC and A Congolese Woman Chief (Mfumu-Mkento)

- The Congo RDC Et la Femme Dirigeante (Mfumu-Nkento)

- The Congo RDC and Congolese Tradition Law (first edition)

- The Congo RDC and Congolese Comedy/Novels

1. *A Mysterious Boy called Timo Mikwaya Well known as Kamina*

2. *Mr. Aleyi-Atondi*

How can this man live with his In-laws for over 15 years?

3. *A Western Professor with an African University Student (Abelengezi)*

4. *Experience of two African young ladies in America (Magoke)*

By

Bepona Collection

Africa presents the Congo RDC and

Experience of Two Young African Ladies in America

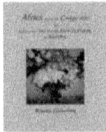

Mr. Aleyi Atondi
How can this man live with his in-laws for over 15 years?

Africa Presents the Congo RDC And
Western Prof. & African Student

ABOUT BEPONA COLLECTION

Our books are written by American of the African descents, particularly from the Congo RDC, who have been compelled to share the Congolese culture with those individuals who are interested in diversity.

Our novels are practically, narrative non-fiction. The names of the characters including the original settings have been withheld intentionally, in order to protect the privacy or identities of the individuals concerned.

All our books are written in simple language, terms and style. Our goal is to share our culture and to express ourselves, but not to impress our readers.

www.ingramcontent.com/pod-product-compliance
Lightning Source LLC
Chambersburg PA
CBHW071430090426
42737CB00011B/1618